CITYSPOTS
LEIPZ

WHAT'S IN YOUR GUIDEBOOK?

Independent authors Impartial up-to-date information from our travel experts, who meticulously source local knowledge.

Experience Thomas Cook's 165 years in the travel industry and guidebook publishing enriches every word with expertise you can trust.

Travel know-how Contributions by thousands of staff around the globe, each one living and breathing travel.

Editors Travel-publishing professionals, pulling everything together to craft a perfect blend of words, pictures, maps and design.

You, the traveller We deliver a practical, no-nonsense approach to information, geared to how you really use it.

CITYSPOTS
LEIPZIG

Kerry Walker

Written by Kerry Walker
Original photography by Christopher Holt
Front cover photography (University Tower) © Jorg Greuel/Getty Images
Series design based on an original concept by Studio 183 Limited

Produced by Cambridge Publishing Management Limited
Project Editor: Penny Isaac
Layout: Trevor Double
Maps: PC Graphics
Transport map: © Communicarta Limited

Published by Thomas Cook Publishing
A division of Thomas Cook Tour Operations Limited
Company Registration No. 1450464 England
PO Box 227, Unit 18, Coningsby Road
Peterborough PE3 8SB, United Kingdom
email: books@thomascook.com
www.thomascookpublishing.com
+ 44 (0) 1733 416477
ISBN-13: 978-184157-750-0

First edition © 2007 Thomas Cook Publishing
Text © 2007 Thomas Cook Publishing
Maps © 2007 Thomas Cook Publishing
Series Editor: Kelly Anne Pipes
Project Editor: Karen Fitzpatrick
Production/DTP: Steven Collins

Printed and bound in Spain by GraphyCems

CONTENTS

SYMBOLS KEY

The following symbols are used throughout this book:

 address   telephone   fax   website address   email   opening times   public transport connections

The following symbols are used on the maps:

information office		O	city
airport		O	large town
hospital		○	small town
police station		=	motorway
bus station		—	main road
railway station			minor road
cathedral		—	railway

● numbers denote featured cafés & restaurants

Hotels and restaurants are graded by approximate price as follows:

£ budget   ££ mid-range   £££ expensive

● *Old meets new in Leipzig's city centre*

INTRODUCING
Leipzig

Introduction

Saxony's Sleeping Beauty has awoken from its communist slumber and is staging its comeback as one of Europe's hottest cities. One-time home to such luminaries as Bach, Goethe and Wagner, Germany's eastern gem has returned to its cultural roots, showcasing cabaret in secluded courtyards and music in sublime concert halls. For classical music, art and comedy fans, the love affair with Leipzig begins here.

But with the tide of tradition come the waves of innovation. Bright-eyed and bushy-tailed, this 500,000-strong university city bubbles over with avant-garde architecture, funky cafés, modern malls and all-night parties. From caipirinhas by the canals in red-bricked Plagwitz to Michael Fischer-Art's multicoloured murals, Leipzig blends cultural clout with cutting edge. There's an undeniable whiff of energy and excitement in the air.

Leipzig wears its riches well: cobbled squares and Gothic spires, boutique-lined arcades and museums creaking under the weight of their treasures, never-ending parks and cavernous cellars are ripe for the picking. Whether you want to join the cheery locals for an alfresco coffee break, hear Bach's cantatas in St Thomas's Church or dance till dawn on Barfussgässchen, this is the place. Waving the flag as Europe's cheapest city, you can live it up for very little in Leipzig.

Stepping away from the centre, Gohlis beckons with its immaculate art nouveau townhouses, while Plagwitz revamps the industrial landscape with gondola rides on its tree-fringed waterways. Leipzig goes green in Rosental's peaceful heathland

and the Auenwald floodplain forest, making it easy to escape the city's throngs.

Linger longer to unravel Halle's clutch of baroque buildings and medieval castles strung along the River Saale. The UNESCO World Heritage Site of Dessau-Wörlitz Gartenrêich sprouts manicured gardens and rococo palaces. Here you can revel in the splendour of royalty, bike through acres of greenery and be inspired by Bauhaus creations – all just a stone's throw away from Leipzig.

⏶ *Bach is one of the city's famous sons*

When to go

SEASONS & CLIMATE

Leipzig is not one for meteorological extremes. The city has a moderate climate, with summers not too hot, peaking at around 25°C (72°F) and winters not too cold; the temperature rarely dips below 0°C (32°F). Spring temperatures hover between 10°C and 15°C (48°F and 56°F): this is the time to enjoy Rosental Park and the Botanical Gardens in bloom.

Leipzig basks in sunshine from June to August, but also gets its fair share of rain, so come prepared for sudden downpours. If you're planning on hiking the Auenwald forest, autumn is a safe bet with mild, dry days. This is also when culture hits its high,

⬤ *Relaxing in the balmy climate*

with events such as the Laughter Fair and Jazz Days taking audiences by storm. Wrap up warm in winter to explore Leipzig's illuminated Christmas Market, one of Germany's finest.

ANNUAL EVENTS

March

Leipzig Book Fair Bury your head in books at Leipzig's celebration of the written word. Expect readings, lectures and debates at this important literary event.

ⓐ Messe-Allee 1 ❶ 0341 678 8240
ⓦ www.leipziger-buchmesse.de

April–May

***A Capella* Festival** Artists stretch their vocal chords at this musical highlight, staging everything from polyphonic song to vocal jazz in churches and concert halls across the city.

ⓦ www.a-cappella-festival.de ⓔ info@a-cappella-festival.de

June

Bach Festival Leipzig pulls the stops out for this ten-day festival of orchestral highs, dedicated to the city's most famous past resident, Johann Sebastian Bach.

❶ 0341 91 37 05 ❶ 0341 91 37 105 ⓦ www.bach-leipzig.de
ⓔ info@bach-leipzig.de

Wave Gothic Meeting Leipzig reveals its darker side at this huge Gothic meeting, featuring open-air concerts, exhibitions, theatre and late-night parties.

❶ 0341 212 0862 ⓦ www.wave-gotik-treffen.de
ⓔ info@wave-gotik-treffen.de

July

Saxonia International Balloon Fiesta Going up! Leipzig looks to the skies as hundreds of balloons float above the city at this five-day summer festival. As well as a whole lotta hot air, there are fireworks and plenty of family attractions.

🕿 0341 868 050 🌐 www.balloons.de

August

Honky Tonk Pub Festival Feel the rhythm at Europe's biggest pub festival. One ticket gains you entry to a range of musical delights, from salsa to swing, in pubs, bars and clubs all over the city.

🕿 0341 303 7300 📠 0341 303 7333 🌐 http://honky-tonk.de

October

International Documentary Film Festival Cutting-edge documentaries, shorts and animation from across the globe draw film buffs to this week-long festival.

🕿 0341 308 640 🌐 www.dokfestival-leipzig.de

📧 info@dok-leipzig.de

Jazz Days The sound of the saxophone jazzes up this funky autumn festival, where up-and-coming talents share the stage with well-known performers.

🌐 www.jazzclub-leipzig.de

Laughter Fair Leipzig loves to laugh at this festival featuring the cream of the comedy crop. Giggle and guffaw at German and international stand-up acts and cabaret. 🕿 0341 87 80 570

📠 0341 87 80 573 🌐 www.lachmesse.de

November
Euro-Scene Festival All the world's a stage at this dramatic six-day festival, staging plays, premieres and improvised theatre in Leipzig's top venues.
☎ 0341 980 0284 🖷 0341 980 4860 🌐 www.euro-scene.de

December
Christmas Market The world's biggest advent calendar, brass bands, an open-air ice rink and 260 stalls selling festive goodies make this one of Leipzig's must-be-there attractions.
☎ 0341 710 4260 🌐 www.leipzig.de

PUBLIC HOLIDAYS
Official public holidays in Saxony
New Year's Day (Neujahrstag) 1 January
Epiphany (Heilige Drei Könige) 6 January
Good Friday (Karfreitag) March/April
Easter Monday (Ostermontag) March/April
Labour Day (Maifeiertag) 1 May
Ascension Day (Christi Himmelfahrt) May
Whit Monday (Pfingstmontag) May/June
Day of Unity (Tag der deutschen Einheit) 3 October
Day of Reformation (Reformationstag) 31 October
Repentance Day (Buß- und Bettag) November
Christmas Day (Erster Weihnachtstag) 25 December
Boxing Day (Zweiter Weihnachtstag) 26 December

The world's biggest advent calendar dominates the Christmas Market

LEIPZIG CHRISTMAS MARKET

Leipzig's month-long Christmas market breathes seasonal cheer into the centre, with Christmas trees and glowing fairy lights. Dating back to 1767, the market hums with carol singers, carousels and the world's largest freestanding advent calendar. Measuring a mammoth 857 sq m (9,225 sq ft), the super-sized calendar on Bottchergasse is one every child would love to have on their wall. Ensure you're there at 16.30 between 1 and 24 December to watch one of the huge doors being opened.

Even Scrooge would melt at the sight of the nativity scene on Augustusplatz, where a flock of real sheep are brought in for the occasion – bah humbug indeed! A focal point of the festivities, this square shrinks beneath a 20-m

(66-ft) giant of a Christmas tree, bedecked in thousands of tiny lights. Kids are kept entertained, slipping and sliding across the open-air ice rink or visiting Father Christmas at the glittering winter wonderland complete with Finnish reindeer.

Feeling peckish? Little wonder with the Christmassy whiff of *Glühwein* (mulled wine) and fresh pretzels tempting on every corner. Taste sugary specialities such as *Pulsnitzer Pfefferkuchen* (chocolate-coated gingerbread) and *Leipziger Räbchen* (cinnamon doughnuts filled with plums and marzipan). All this may seem like an adventure in cholesterol, but who cares, it's Christmas!

If it is gifts you're after, there are more than 260 stalls encouraging you to loosen your purse strings. Look out for the hand-carved decorations, incense smokers, nativity pyramids, wooden crib figures and brightly coloured nutcrackers from the Erzgebirge mountains.

Musical highlights of this yuletide event include brass band concerts in front of the Opera House on Augustusplatz and the renowned Thomaner Choir (St Thomas's Boys Choir), which has a history dating back nearly 800 years, performing at St Thomas's Church. To feel the true spirit of Christmas, take a peek at around 800 intricate nativity scenes on display in the Old Town Hall. The festivities culminate just before Christmas Eve with a spectacular parade and concert in the city centre. ① 0341 710 4260 ⓦ www.leipzig.de ⓛ 10.00–20.00 Sun–Thur, 10.00–21.00 Fri–Sat

History

A city with a turbulent past, Leipzig is now looking towards a brilliant future. With a strategic location between Eastern and Western Europe, the city has been marked by many changes and foreign influences over the ages, and has played a pivotal role in shaping the history of Saxony and Germany.

While Leipzig's roots stretch back as far as the 7th century, when Slavic settlers occupied the banks of the Elster and Parthe rivers, the city was first mentioned in writing in 1015 in the Bishop Thietmar von Merseburg's chronicle. In 1165, the city was granted 'market rights'; two trade fairs a year were held, sparking off a period of unparalleled growth which saw Leipzig become one of Europe's most important trade routes.

In 1409 the University of Leipzig was founded, and the city began to prosper and progress as a centre of law and the publishing industry. A key milestone was achieved in 1481 when Leipzig's first book was printed by Marcus Brandis, and in 1519 Leipzig became the centre of European attention when the leader of the Protestant Reformation, Martin Luther, denied the divine right of the pope in the dramatic Leipzig Debate. Leipzig accepted the Reformation in 1539.

The 17th century brought a mixture of tragedy and triumph for Leipzig. Battles fought at Breitenfeld and Lützen during the Thirty Years War (1618–48) left a trail of destruction and disease in their wake. Yet at the same time the city thrived as a centre of academic excellence. The world's first-ever newspaper was printed here in 1650 and the city was home to gifted men such as philosopher and mathematician Gottfried Wilhelm von

Leibnitz and composer Johann Sebastian Bach, cantor at St Thomas's Church from 1723 until his death.

The University of Leipzig reached its literary peak in the 18th century, shining with illustrious scholars such as Schiller, Gellert and Goethe, who studied law from the age of 16 and wrote many of his early plays and poems in the city. The Auerbachs Keller restaurant is mentioned in his drama *Faust*.

In 1813, Prussian forces defeated Napoleon's troops at the Battle of Leipzig. The Monument to the Battle of the Nations commemorates the many thousands that lost their lives in the battle. On a more positive note, Leipzig gave rise to some of the world's greatest composers in the 19th century, including Felix Mendelssohn, Robert Schumann and Richard Wagner, who established musical academies and concert halls such as the Leipzig Conservatory and Gewandhaus.

A spurt of growth in the early 20th century was brought to a sudden halt with the advent of World War II (1939–45): thousands of Jewish residents were killed and much of the city was reduced to rubble in the 1943 bombings. After the war, unrest bubbled under the city's surface until in 1989 Leipzig's Monday demonstrations evolved into the biggest protest ever against the East German regime, ultimately leading to the downfall of the communist government and German reunification in 1990.

Positive and confident, today's Leipzig is looking good, thanks to an economic boom which has been fuelled, among other factors, by the opening of the Porsche (2002) and BMW (2005) car manufacturing plants. The city hosted five football matches in the FIFA World Cup 2006.

Lifestyle

The only way is up for Leipzig. With its futuristic trade fair, glittering malls and revolutionary art centres, it's hard to believe this city was caught in the clutches of communism just two decades ago. Today, Leipzig has risen like a phoenix from the communist ashes and is growing leaps and bounds in culture, industry and business. Tie that with the kick it got out of the FIFA World Cup 2006, a resounding success, and you are looking at a city that feels confident and comfortable in its own skin.

And it shows. A glance at the Leipzig locals confirms they are an easy-going and down-to-earth bunch who know how to enjoy themselves. They make no secret of their passion for music – which you'll hear on every street corner; art in every shape and form; partying (as a blurry-eyed night out on Barfussgässchen will confirm), and sport – football and athletics to be exact. Strike up a conversation on any one of these topics and you're bound to get a good response. Most inhabitants speak English, but test out your German if you want to impress.

Buzzing and free-spirited, Leipzig's 16,700 students give the city a forward-looking, multicultural feel that is welcoming to travellers. While its baroque, Renaissance and art nouveau architecture may scream 'traditional', this liberal city has a rebellious streak and a passion for the peculiar. It's impossible not to feel relaxed in a place where Goths and lawyers chew the cud over coffee, or punks and academics philosophise over a glass of gold-hued Gose beer. A melting pot of cultures and subcultures, this is one place where you really can come as you are.

CHILDREN OF THE REVOLUTION

Daring and defiant, Leipzig has never been afraid to stand up for what it believes in. Nikolaikirche was at the centre of the peaceful Monday demonstrations in 1989, where thousands flocked to pray for peace. The movement spread to other German cities, culminating in the events of 9 October 1989, when 70,000 people took to the streets to demonstrate against the communist regime, with the famous chant *Wir sind das Volk* ('we are the people'). Just a month later, the Berlin Wall came down and paved the way for German reunification.

◔ *Music forms a backbeat to this exciting city*

Culture

Leipzig doesn't just display its culture behind glass: it lives and breathes it. Having been home to the likes of Bach, Wagner and Mendelssohn, it's little wonder music and art run through this city's veins. But Leipzig is supportive of the underdog, too, making waves with innovative and inspiring art forms, where fresh talent shares the spotlight with well-known luminaries. Moving from free violin concertos on Thomaskirchhof Square to Michael Fischer-Art's open-air creations, this is one city where you don't have to spend money to enjoy cultural delights.

For classical highs, see Leipzig's acclaimed orchestra perform in the frescoed Gewandhaus on Augustusplatz, or cross the square to the Opera House for opera, musicals and ballet. At weekends, Thomaskirche resonates to the spine-tingling sound of famous choirs – among them the resident St Thomas's Boys Choir performing Bach's cantatas. Even the Schiller House in Gohlis gets in on the act, staging garden concerts in summer.

Visitors who enjoy a laugh and understand a little German should make sure they catch one of Leipzig's superb cabaret and variety shows. At the forefront of satirical and stand-up comedy, venues such as Pfeffermühle, Frosch and Kabarett Academixer stage regular performances in centuries-old buildings and courtyards. For the linguistically challenged, Krystallpalast Varieté offers an eclectic programme featuring everything from contortionists to gravity-defying trapeze artists.

Improvised art and jam sessions are at their best in the underground vaults of the red-brick Mortizbastei, a popular

⬥ *The opera house is part of a vibrant cultural scene*

student haunt set around a central courtyard. If you like your art raw and edgy, venture further south to check out the offerings at Werk II, a revamped factory churning out alternative plays, concerts and films. Another offbeat one to watch out for is naTo, hosting wacky events alongside jazz sessions, arthouse films and modern dance productions.

The glass-walled DBK (Museum of Fine Arts) houses German Expressionism – glimpse Max Klinger's *Beethoven* – plus Dutch Masters and Impressionist works by artists such as Rodin. More modern pieces grace the walls of the Contemporary Art Gallery and the maze-like Baumwollspinnerei, housed in a former cotton mill. To be literally surrounded by art, check out Yadegar Asisi's striking 360° panoramas in the Asisi Factory Panometer – certain to raise eyebrows.

THE DARLING OF DARING ART

Walking around Leipzig, you can't fail to notice Michael Fischer-Art's in-your-face colours and larger-than-life characters, often splashed against the sides of public buildings. The Leipzig-born artist is not shy when it comes to wielding his paintbrush to create bold and bright designs that are magnets to contemporary art lovers. Opposite the Fine Arts Museum, his surreal murals have given new life to the Drei Türme, three derelict concrete tower blocks on Brühl, which are now quite a shock to the senses!

▶ *Markt – Market Square – forms the hub of Leipzig*

Shopping

From original boutiques to art deco antiques, Leipzig keeps avid shoppers on their toes. Dip into the city centre's pockets to uncover high-street stores and glass-walled malls, old-world arcades and markets with mountains of seasonal produce.

Leipzig's shops are open year-round, six days a week. Shopping hours are generally 10.00–19.00 Monday to Friday and 10.00–16.00 Saturday, although major shopping malls like the Hauptbahnhof at Leipzig's main station stay open daily until 22.00.

Fashionistas seeking the latest styles make for Peters Strasse, Grimmaische Strasse and Neumarkt, where department store giant Galeria Kaufhof is an enjoyable one-stop shop. Unique gifts such as wooden Erzgebirge decorations and Meissener porcelain fill the speciality shops that huddle around Markt and Naschmarkt. Eagle-eyed collectors sniff out antiques and second-hand books in Katharinen Strasse.

Leipzig is punctuated with elegant arcades. Topping the shop-and-stroll list is the partly Renaissance, partly art nouveau Mädler Passage, housing smart boutiques including Lacoste, Armani and crystal-studded Swarovski. With its frescoes and hidden courtyards, the elegant Specks Hof arcade is the place to spend on fine wines and original art. Another favourite is Barthels Hof, peppered with dinky boutiques selling handcrafted jewellery and hats.

You'll find 140 shops, restaurants and cafés beneath the Promenaden Hauptbahnhof's glass roof. Big names like Mango, Yves Rocher, Swatch and Esprit cluster here, plus souvenir shops, bookshops and a handful of designer boutiques. Pick up funky footwear and sweet treats in the ultra-modern Petersbogen mall opposite the new town hall.

If you want markets, Leipzig has plenty to offer. Stalls are piled high with fresh produce such as fruit, cheese, honey and wholemeal breads every Tuesday and Friday at Leipzig's food market (09.00–17.00). Find bric-a-brac at the flea market on

● *Flex your credit card in the Mädler Passage*

the first weekend of the month and hidden gems at the antique market on the last. Time your visit to buy beautiful blooms at May's flower market, local brews at July's Beer Exchange, or hand-carved decorations and gingerbread at December's Christmas market.

For a lingering taste of Leipzig, take home cream-filled *Bachpfeiffen* chocolates from Arko in the Mädler Passage and coin-shaped *Bachtaler* pralines from Café Kandler. Wrap and pack delicate Meissen porcelain, Gose beer (and the glass to match), and hand-carved Christmas decorations from Heidrich & Zeidler.

USEFUL SHOPPING PHRASES

What time do the shops open/close?
Um wieviel Uhr öffnen/schließen die Geschäfte?
Oom veefeel oor erffnen/shleessen dee geshefter?

How much is this?
Wieviel kostet das?
Veefeel kostet das?

Can I try this on?
Kann ich das anprobieren?
Can ikh das anprobeeren?

My size is ...
Ich habe Größe . . .
Ikh haber grerser . . .

I'll take this one, thank you
Ich nehme das, danke schön
Ikh neymer das, danker shern

This is too large/too small/too expensive
Es ist zu groß/zu klein/zu teuer
Es ist tsu gross/tsu kline/tsu toyer

Eating & drinking

Both the food and the prices are appetising in Leipzig, whipping up traditional, world and new-wave flavours. Go underground to savour Saxon fare in wood-panelled cellars serving a slice of history. Swim a little deeper into the city's gastro waters to fish out art nouveau brasseries, minimalist-style sushi bars and fusion cuisine.

DINING DISTRICTS

In the centre, tuck into hearty local dishes in centuries-old taverns and vaulted cellars on Thomaskirchhof Square, Hain Strasse and the narrow streets fanning out from the market square. Barfussgässchen, Burg Strasse and Nikolai Strasse tempt with everything from shark steaks to filling falafels. With terraces on the cobblestones and pretty hidden courtyards, summer here spells alfresco dining with a Mediterranean feel.

Low-key and un-touristy, Gohlis comes first for affordable romance, fine dining and Gose beer, blending high-ceilinged art nouveau restaurants, intimate trattorias and snug gastro pubs.

PRICE RATING

The restaurant price guides used in this book indicate the average cost of a three-course meal for one person, excluding drinks.

£ up to €20   ££ between €20 and €35
£££ more than €35

Wald Strasse boasts restaurants serving ethnic dishes such as spicy tacos and Thai curries, while Gohliser Strasse scores points for authentic French and local treats.

The south sizzles with quirky little restaurants, relaxed pubs and arty cafés with a boho vibe. Head for canalside Plagwitz to dine by the water's edge or in converted red-brick factories. Südvorstadt's Karl-Liebknecht-Strasse and Münzgasse have a generous sprinkling of global flavours – from cheap-and-cheerful Chinese to Lebanese offerings.

FOOD MARKETS

Every Tuesday and Friday (09.00–17.00), local farmers set up shop on Markt (Market Square) and stalls overflow with tasty organic produce. This is the place to sniff out pungent cheeses, shiny fruit and vegetables, fresh fish and meat, crusty homemade breads, and pretty much whatever else takes your fancy.

LOCAL SPECIALITIES

For a true taste of Leipzig, munch on regional dishes that use simple but flavoursome ingredients. A favourite is *Leipziger Allerlei* (vegetable stew with crayfish tails and flour dumplings), washed back with citrusy Müller-Thurgau wines or tangy Gose beer. A meal is often rounded off with plenty of coffee, or *Scheelchen Heessen* as it's called locally.

Leipzig's array of pastries and pralines make mouths water and waistlines expand, so indulge now and diet tomorrow. The sweet-toothed should try *Leipziger Lerche* cakes, marzipan-and-plum stuffed *Leipziger Räbchen* dough balls rolled in cinnamon

LARKING AROUND

You're bound to see the *Leipziger Lerche* (Leipzig Lark) on the menu at some point. This tasty speciality dates back to the 18th century when the dish was made with skylarks. Having developed a taste for songbirds, the locals would hunt migrating larks on the Elbe and Saale rivers in autumn, wrap them in bacon and serve them with sauerkraut. The practice was outlawed by the king of Saxony in 1876, following public protest, but a sweet version still exists. It is an entirely bird-free delight: a delicious cake made with shortcrust pastry, almonds, nuts and strawberry jam.

and *Quarkkeulchen* curd dumplings. Putting the culture into confectionery are *Bachpfeiffen*, coffee-coated pralines filled with cream and shaped like organ pipes, made in tribute to Bach.

PICNIC SPOTS

Leipzig has rich pickings in the picnic department. When the weather warms, fill your basket with local specialities and make for shady spots like Clara-Zetkin and Rosental parks. Lay your blanket on Lake Cospuden's beach or the Karl Heine Canal's banks. The Dübener Heide's wild heathlands and Auenwald woodlands offer a back-to-nature experience.

TIPPING

Many of Leipzig's restaurants, cafés and bars include a service charge in the bill, but it's normal to leave a small tip if you were pleased with the service. Locals usually round the bill off to the nearest euro or leave a tip of around five per cent for good or ten per cent for excellent service. In Germany, it's standard practice to tip waiters and waitresses when paying the bill, not by leaving the money on the table.

USEFUL DINING PHRASES

I would like a table for ... people
Ein Tisch für ... Personen, bitte
Ine teesh foor ... perzohnen, bitter

Waiter/waitress!
Herr Ober/Fräulein, bitte!
Hair ohber/froyline, bitter!

May I have the bill, please?
Die Rechnung, bitte?
Dee rekhnung, bitter?

I am a vegetarian. Does this contain meat?
Ich bin Vegetarier (Vegetarierin fem.). Enthält das hier Fleisch?
Ish bin veggetaareer (veggetaareerin). Enthelt dass heer flyshe?

Where is the toilet (restroom) please?
Wo sind die Toiletten, bitte?
Voo zeent dee toletten, bitter?

I would like a cup of/two cups of/another coffee/tea
Eine Tasse/Zwei Tassen/noch eine Tasse Kaffee/Tee, bitte
Ikh merkhter iner tasser/tsvy tassen kafey/tey, bitter

I would like a beer/two beers, please
Ein Bier/Zwei Biere, bitte
Ine beer/tsvy beerer, bitter

Entertainment & nightlife

When most cities start to snooze, Leipzig lets its hair down. Fuelled by late-night revellers and party-mad students, plenty of cheap drinks and late licensing in the wall-to-wall bars and clubs, this sleepless city has one of Germany's hippest and most active after-dark scenes.

The secret is its diversity – you can step from Bach cantatas in cobbled courtyards and cocktails on Barfussgässchen to salsa moves in Südvorstadt and mellow grooves in canal-crossed Plagwitz. Or how about an evening with a twist? Leipzig's passion for the weird and wonderful has seen kooky bars sprout up: you can sip mojitos lying on the floor at Sol y Mar, or watch others have their hair snipped at Nova Barocca.

Bracing themselves for a big night, most locals begin the evening with a few drinks in the centre to gather momentum. The night kicks off around 23.00 when the bars lining Barfussgässchen fill up to bursting point. If you want to hit the clubs, don't get there before midnight unless you want the dance floor to yourself. There's plenty of time to strut your stuff before breakfast!

Leipzig's cultural cup runs over and you will not be stuck for entertainment: it boasts theatres, concert halls, cinemas, cabaret clubs and avant-garde arts venues. From satirical comics to soprano singers, you're well catered for here. To book tickets in advance, contact the venue direct or try **Ticket Shop**, covering major festivals, gigs and performances.
ⓐ Arndtstrasse 10 ⓣ 0341 980 0098 ⓦ www.lvz-ticket.de

Bars & pubs

The epicentre of the Drallewatsch pub mile – the narrow
Barfussgässchen – feels Mediterranean, with music pumping
out of every bar and alfresco drinking on the heated terraces.
At weekends, the bars and basement clubs are loud and
lively, so you'll often have to squeeze your way through
the door. The theatre district around Gottsched Strasse scores

● *Barrels and bratwurst in the Auerbachs Keller*

points for its cult bars, quirky cafés and stand-up comedy, while Gohlis tempts those seeking Gose beer in snug, wood-panelled taverns.

King of the alternative scene, Südvorstadt's Karl-Liebknecht-Strasse has a come-as-you-are feel that reels in the students. Expect everything from gothic cellars to psychedelic pubs in which DJs still spin vinyl. Nearby, the pub mile around Münzgasse and Petersssteinweg is chock-a-block with laid-back lounge bars that don't feel much bigger than a postage stamp. For a boho atmosphere, canal views and beer in converted red-brick factories, make for Plagwitz.

Clubs

Clubbers that want to dance till dawn head for the area in and around Barfussgässchen, where nightspots range from kitsch to ultra-cool. Names to look out for include basement jazz club Spizz, and Saxony's so-called biggest ski chalet, Alpenmax. Go south for infectious merengue and bachata rhythms at Cuban Club Havana.

Performing arts

Illuminated by night, Leipzig's two performing arts giants the Gewandhaus and Opera House dominate either side of the sprawling Augustusplatz. This is also the site for plenty of open-air events like the free Classic Open festival in August, where classical, jazz and blues stars take to the stage and wow the crowds. For an offbeat experience, check out the programme at the arty Mortizbastei, Pfeffermühle or Kabarett Academixer.

The following websites feature more information about
entertainment and nightlife in Leipzig:

Leipzig Tag & Nacht gives the lowdown on Leipzig's hippest
bars, clubs and restaurants. Ⓦ www.leipzigtagundnacht.de

Z-Leipzig Online has the latest listings for Leipzig festivals, gigs,
parties, theatre productions, film screenings and club nights.
Ⓦ www.z-leipzig-nachts.de

⬤ *All ages can enjoy outdoor pursuits*

Sport & relaxation

SPECTATOR SPORTS

The jewel in the crown of football-mad Saxony, Leipzig has been having a ball ever since VfB Leipzig won the cup at the first German championship in 1903. Built to shine for the FIFA World Cup 2006, the state-of-the-art Central Stadium can squeeze 45,000 spectators onto its terraces, but you should book in advance to secure tickets to the big matches.

Just next door, Leipzig Arena reveals the city's passion for athletics. The multipurpose venue has been in the limelight with top events like the World Boxing Championships. It is, perhaps, one of the only places where you can see judo tournaments and world-class jazz concerts under the same roof.

Stepping south, Scheibenholz Racecourse has a 140-year-old horse racing history and picks up speed during the summer season (May to October).

PARTICIPATION SPORTS
Swimming

When weather permits, take the plunge in Lake Kulkwitz's clean waters and open-air pools, or swim laps in Leipzig's Kleinzschocher and Gohlis lidos surrounded by greenery. No matter in which direction you head, you won't have to go far before you reach one of the city's many indoor pools.

Walking & cycling

Leipzig's plethora of parks and gardens, Lake Kulkwitz's promenade and the canal-crossed Auenwald floodplain forest are prime two-wheel and two-leg territory. Spiralling out from green spaces like the Clara Zetkin Park and Botanical Gardens, walkers and cyclists can enjoy more than 200 km (124 miles) of marked trails. Bike hire is available at the main station.

Watersports

Daredevils get their white-water thrills on dune-fringed Lake Cospuden just south of Leipzig. Spanning 420 hectares (1.6 sq miles), the lake has a watersports centre, where those with the nerve can scuba-dive beneath the water or kite-surf above it. Even wetter and wilder is the nearby Markkleeberg Kanupark, where you can test out hydrospeed rafting or freestyle canoeing.

❶ 0341 356 510 ⓦ www.cospuden.de ⓔ info@cospuden.de

RELAXATION

Spa

After all that strenuous exercise, why not head for Markkleeberg's lakefront saunas and solaria: the perfect antidote for aching muscles. For the ultimate unwind just ten minutes' walk east of the centre, make for Sachsen Therme's warren of 100°C (192°F) saunas, steamy whirlpools and treatment rooms.

ⓐ Schongauer Strasse 191 ❶ 0341 710 770 ❶ 0341 259 9925
ⓦ www.sachsentherme.de ⓔ email@sachsen-therme.de
Ⓝ Tram: 7

Accommodation

Whether your preference is for funky backpacker digs or grand 19th-century villas, Leipzig has accommodation to suit all tastes and budgets. If your budget is limited, choose no-frills hostels in the centre or family-run guesthouses with bags of character just a short tram ride away. For those with a little cash to spare, try contemporary hotels with original art or five-star spa hotels for the ultimate unwind.

HOTELS

Am Ratsholz £f Unwind in the sauna at this contemporary hotel. Comfortable rooms all have cable TV, direct-dial phone, safe and fully equipped kitchenette. ⓐ Anton-Zickmantel-Strasse 44 ⓣ 0341 494 4500 ⓦ www.hotel-am-ratsholz.de ⓔ hotel.am.ratsholz@t-online.de ⓥ Tram: 3, 13

Hotel Berlin £f Relax in the shady courtyard of this hotel near the Völkerschlachtdenkmal. The restaurant serves a generous breakfast buffet. Guests enjoy free parking. ⓐ Riebeckstrasse 30 ⓣ 0341 267 3000 ⓦ www.hotel-berlin-leipzig.de ⓔ hotel-berlin-leipzig@t-online.de ⓥ Tram: 4

PRICE RATING
The ratings below indicate the approximate cost of a room for two people for one night
£ under €45   ££ €45–€80   £££ €80 and above

Hotel Garni ££ Put your feet up at this centrally located, three-star hotel near the opera house. The bright apartments have balconies. Ask the friendly, English-speaking staff for information on Leipzig attractions and bike hire. ⓐ Gerichtsweg 12 ⓣ 0341 12780 ⓕ 0341 127 8700 ⓦ www.leipzig-hotel-garni.de ⓝ Tram: 4, 7

Hotel Merseburger Hof ££ This turreted, red-and-white brick hotel oozes old-world grandeur. The plush rooms decked out in greens and creams offer mod cons like wireless internet access. Tuck into Saxon specialities in the restaurant and enjoy the onsite bowling alley. ⓐ Merseburger Strasse 107 ⓣ 0341 477 4462 ⓕ 0341 477 4413 ⓔ info@merseburger-hof.de ⓦ www.merseburger-hof.de ⓝ Tram: 7

Vivaldi Hotel ££ This Italian-style hotel is a home away from home. Snug rooms with sleek drapes and chunky wood furniture have cable TV, wireless internet access and minibar. Chill out in the courtyard restaurant. ⓐ Wittenberger Strasse 87 ⓣ 0341 903 60 ⓕ 0341 903 6234 ⓦ www.hotel-vivaldi.de ⓝ Tram: 16

Accento £££ This funky hotel provides a breath of fresh air with its Pop Art design and modern fitness centre with sauna. Expect rooms with bold colours and smooth contours. ⓐ Tauchaer Strasse 260 ⓣ 0341 52460 ⓦ www.accento-hotel.de ⓔ welcome@accento-hotel.de ⓝ Tram: 9

Galerie Hotel Leipziger Hof £££ Discover the art of sleeping at this tranquil hotel doubling up as a gallery with 200 original works. Guests can unwind in the whirlpool, sauna and beer garden. ⓐ Hedwigstrasse 1–3 ⓣ 0341 69740 ⓕ 0341 697 4150 ⓦ www.leipziger-hof.de ⓔ info@leipziger-hof.de ⓝ Tram: 1, 3

Günnewig Hotel Vier Jahreszeiten £££ Expect a warm welcome at this cheery hotel near the station, where Leipzig's attractions are on your doorstep. Spacious, spotless rooms have comfy beds and WiFi access. Enjoy a hearty breakfast buffet in the light-filled conservatory. ⓐ Kurt-Schumacher-Strasse 23–29 ⓣ 0341 985 10 ⓕ 0341 985 122 ⓦ www.guennewig.de ⓔ vier.jahreszeiten@guennewig.de ⓝ Train: main station

⬢ Take in the sights from a city centre hotel

Hotel Fürstenhof Leipzig £££ Blow the budget at Leipzig's most opulent hotel. This palatial building is all floor-to-ceiling glass, high ceilings and chandeliers. The icing on the five-star cake is the AquaMarin spa, with a landscaped pool and Roman steam bath. ⓐ Troendlinring 8 ⓣ 0341 1400 ⓕ 0341 140 3700 ⓦ www.starwoodhotels.com ⓔ fuerstenhof.leipzig@arabellasheraton.com ⓝ Tram: 1, 4, 12

Hotel Michaelis £££ Small but perfectly formed, this lovingly restored listed building is a find. Rooms have satellite TV and minibar. Savour Mediterranean flavours in the terrace restaurant. ⓐ Paul-Gruner-Strasse 44 ⓣ 0341 26780 ⓦ www.hotel-michaelis.de ⓔ hotel-michaelis@t-online.de ⓝ Tram: 10, 11

HOSTELS

Central Globetrotter £ Just minutes from Leipzig's central station, this hostel has clean two- to eight-bed dorms. Facilities feature a communal kitchen, lockers, internet access and bar. ⓐ Kurt-Schumacher-Strasse 41 ⓣ 0341 149 8960 ⓕ 0341 149 8962 ⓦ www.globetrotter-leipzig.de ⓔ info@globetrotter-leipzig.de ⓝ Train: main station

Hostel Sleep Lion £ The pick of the budget bunch, this laid-back hostel set in an attractive townhouse is in Leipzig's theatre district. Bike hire and internet access are available. ⓐ Käthe-Kollwitz-Strasse 3 ⓣ 0341 993 9480 ⓕ 0341 993 9482 ⓦ www.hostel-leipzig.de ⓔ info@hostel-leipzig.de ⓝ Tram: 1, 14

GUESTHOUSES

Pension Ameta £ A good cheapie, this whitewashed townhouse is close to Clara-Zetkin Park. Light and airy, the self-catering rooms with wood floors and comfy beds have private bathrooms and kitchenettes. ⓐ Fichtestrasse 12 ❶ 0341 330 0000 ⓦ www.ameta-pension.de ⓔ ameta@t-online.de ⓝ Tram: 10, 11

Abtnaundorfer Park ££ This family-run guesthouse housed in an 18th-century villa and surrounded by leafy parkland has its own terrace, gardens and car park. Elegant rooms all have shower, phone, satellite TV and minibar. ⓐ Abtnaundorfer Strasse 61 ❶ 0341 232 7885 ⓦ www.abtnaundorferpark.de ⓔ info@abtnaundorferpark.de ⓝ Tram: 1

CAMPSITES

Camping am Kulkwitzer See £ This peaceful spot overlooking Lake Kulkwitz's clear waters is about 6 km (4 miles) from the centre. Open from May to October, it has a bakery, playground, boat hire and lakeside restaurant. ⓐ Seestrasse 1 ❶ 0341 710 770 ❶ 0341 7107 717 ⓦ www.kulkwitzer-see.de ⓔ info@kulkwitzer-see.de ⓝ Tram: 15

Camping Auensee £ Open year-round, this back-to-nature campsite has 168 pitches in the Auenwald woodlands. Enjoy outdoor activities like cycling and hiking. There is a sports field, children's playground and facilities for guests with special needs. ⓐ Gustav-Esche-Strasse 5 ❶ 0341 465 1600 ❶ 0341 465 1617 ⓦ www.camping-auensee.de ⓝ Bus: 80

THE BEST OF LEIPZIG

Whether you are on a flying visit to Leipzig, or taking a more leisurely break in Germany, the city offers some sights and experiences that should not be missed.

TOP 10 ATTRACTIONS

- **Auerbachs Keller** The whiff of sausages and hum of chatter hit you as you descend the staircase to this vast cellar, where Goethe found inspiration (see pages 72–3).

- **Bach Museum** A symphony of Renaissance romance and Bach melodies, this museum strikes a chord with classical music lovers (see page 61).

- **Thomaskirche** (St Thomas's Church) Glimpse the cross-ribbed vaulting and Gothic nave at this 13th-century church, where Bach once conducted (see page 65).

- **Museum der Bildenden Künste (MDBK)** (Fine Arts Museum) Max Klinger's marble *Beethoven* sculpture and works by Ruisdael and Rubens are amongst the treats at this light-flooded gallery (see page 66).

- **Altes Rathaus** (Town Hall) Trace Leipzig's history behind the walls of this Renaissance edifice on Markt (Market Square) (see pages 60–1).

- **Grassi Museum Complex** This cultural complex shelters a trio of museums, moving from musical instruments to applied art and ethnology (see page 66).

- **Rosental Park** Laze beside the fountains and hike over unspoilt heathland in this central pocket of greenery (see page 92).

- **Leipzig Opera House** Ballet dancers pirouette across the stage and world-class sopranos hit the high notes on Augustusplatz (see page 66).

- **Völkerschlachtdenkmal** (Monument of the Battle of Nations) Towering over Leipzig, this iconic stone giant commemorates the battle fought against Napoleon's forces (see page 80).

- **Gosenschenke Ohne Bedenken** Discover the delights of Leipzig's amber nectar with a glass of citrusy Gose in this wood-panelled cellar (see page 100).

◆ *Cruising on the Karl Heine canal*

HALF-DAY: LEIPZIG IN A HURRY

Stroll past the Renaissance arches of the Alte Rathaus (Old Town Hall) on the cobbled Markt (Market Square), pausing to gaze at the octagonal tower of Nikolaikirche (St Nicholas's Church). Admire Dutch Masters in the MDBK (Fine Arts Museum), before enjoying beer and bratwurst in the 16th-century wood-panelled Auerbachs Keller, where Goethe penned *Faust*.

1 DAY: TIME TO SEE A LITTLE MORE

A whirlwind musical tour takes in the Bach Museum and the 13th-century Thomaskirche (St Thomas's Church), where Bach worked for 27 years as cantor. After a dose of culture in the Grassi Museum's galleries, relax beside the Clara-Zetkin Park's fountains with a picnic, then boutique shop in the elegant Mädler Passage and Specks Hof arcades. Round out your day on a classical high at the Gewandhaus, the glass-walled concert hall.

2–3 DAYS: SHORT CITY BREAK

You've devoured much of what the centre has to offer, so now take a bite out of Leipzig's lesser-known corners. Head south for sweeping panoramas at the Asisi Factory and to see the lofty Monument of the Battle of Nations – climb 90 m (295 ft) to the top to enjoy far-reaching city views. Take time out to hike or bike in the Auenwald forest, swim in Lake Cospuden's clear waters, or scream at the top of your lungs on Belantis Theme Park's roller coasters.

Go west to Plagwitz to boat past red-brick factories on the Karl Heine Canal and soak up the boho vibe in this revamped industrial district. Stepping north, find peace seeing Rosental Park, elephants at the zoo and baroque art at Gohlis Palace.

LONGER: ENJOYING LEIPZIG TO THE FULL

If time is not an issue, linger for a while to savour Leipzig before exploring the region's hidden gems. Northwest of Leipzig, Halle is split in two by the snaking River Saale. Spot the Gothic spires framing the city's skyline, antique instruments in Handel House (the composer's birthplace) and Expressionist works festooning the walls of the red-turreted Moritzburg Castle.

Further north, castle-hop your way around the Dessau-Wörlitz Gartenreich, a UNESCO World Heritage Site graced with rococo palaces, mirror lakes and well-groomed gardens.

◯ *Art nouveau architecture is a feature of the city*

Something for nothing

Rated Europe's cheapest city in the 2006 Worldwide Cost-of-Living Survey, you won't have to dig deep to enjoy Leipzig's riches. Kick off your stay with an amble through the labyrinthine city centre, pausing to soak up the relaxed vibe beside the Renaissance Rathaus in the Markt and take a peek behind the doors of Thomaskirche and Nikolaikirche – it won't cost you a penny (or a euro, to be precise).

Leipzig's high population of music students means the street performers here are practically pros. See them strum and serenade beside the Bach statue on Nikolaikirchhof Square, or take a stroll along Grimmaische Strasse to marvel at buskers, human statues, acrobats and jugglers. Pause for a budget snack from the mobile hotdog man near Galeria Kaufhof, who browns his sausages on a grill strapped to his front!

Trace Leipzig's fascinating history for free in the Stasi Museum, home to the Stasi (secret police) headquarters until 1989. Meanwhile, culture vultures get occasional kicks from complimentary events at the Moritzbastei, Leipzig's thrifty student honey-pot, staging everything from live jazz to improvised theatre (check the programme in advance). Drinks and snacks served here are among the cheapest in town.

It costs nothing to immerse yourself in art nouveau by wandering Waldstrasse in Gohlis, which is lined with row upon row of beautifully restored townhouses. While you're in the mood for walking, go west to Rosental's Tower, which peers above the treetops – the views over Leipzig from the top are worth the climb. Bring along a picnic to make the most of the park's shady picnic areas.

Summer in the city calls for lazy days on the beaches fringing Lake Kulkwitz, 20 minutes to the west of Leipzig, and long hikes in the cool Auenwald floodplain forest. A great alternative to the zoo is Leipzig's wildlife reserve, where you can observe European species like wild boar, elks, owls, lynx and otters in their near-to-natural habitat ① 0341 30330 Ⓦ www.wildpark-leipzig-freunde.de Ⓝ Tram: 9

🔺 *Relive Leipzig's troubled past at the Stasi Museum*

When it rains

With a host of indoor sights and shops, Leipzig never lets a sudden downpour dampen its spirits. When the rain falls, take shelter in one of the city's old-world coffee houses for a caffeine fix with a generous dollop of culture. The sublime Zum Arabischen Coffe Baum has pralines and pastries to take your mind off even the dreariest day. Nearby, Café Kandler, overlooking Thomaskirche, brews creative teas named after great musicians – the ultimate wet-weather pick-me-up.

Shopping? Leipzig's got it covered. First up is the ultra-modern Hauptbahnhof mall, where you can hop from one high-street store to the next before enjoying a warming bowl of organic soup in Soupito or a vitamin-rich juice in Vitamix. If designer labels are more up your street, make for the elegant Mädler Passage arcade, where names like Aigner, Armani and Porsche Design tempt you to splash your cash.

Showers spell happy hours spent exploring Leipzig's top museums and galleries. For classical melodies, instruments and hands-on displays, the Bach Musuem is a must. Allow enough time to take in the extensive collection at the Grassi Museum Complex, spanning everything from hand-carved African artefacts to age-old harps. Those crazy about cars will love Rübesams Da Capo's shiny old-timers in Plagwitz, while bookworms can pore over the well-stocked shelves at the German National Library.

Even when it's cold outside, one place pumping out plenty of warmth is Sachsen Therme spa, where you can forget the drizzle by steaming and inhaling the essential oils (test out the oxygen and eucalyptus saunas), taking a dip in the effervescent whirlpools, or treating yourself to a soothing back scrub and rub. If beer is more your thing than bubbles, snuggle up with a glass of Gose in Ohne Bedenken's wood-panelled cellar or beside the Bayerischer Bahnhof's huge copper vats. Ahhh, a few sips of the amber nectar and suddenly everything looks much brighter!

◔ *The Grassi complex hosts a trio of interesting museums*

On arrival

TIME DIFFERENCES

Like the rest of Germany, Leipzig is on Central European Time (CET), an hour ahead of Greenwich Mean Time (GMT) and two hours ahead during Daylight Savings Time (late Mar–end Oct).

ARRIVING

By air

Located 18 km (11 miles) from the centre, Leipzig-Halle Airport is the base for 25 airlines flying to 60 destinations across Germany and Europe, including Munich, London, Paris, Vienna and Madrid. Air Berlin offers budget deals, operating a daily service to London Stansted, Glasgow and Manchester.

Modern and user-friendly, the airport has an information desk, ATMs and car hire at Terminal B on the ground floor. There are also shops, restaurants, an internet access point, children's play area, florist and bakery.

The airport has good connections to central Leipzig. A speedy train service departs every 30 minutes from 3.50am to 11.50pm for Leipzig and Halle, with the journey taking just 15 minutes. Taxis are readily available from the stand in front of Terminal B and should set you back around €15. ⓐ Leipzig/Halle Airport 1 ⓘ 0341 224 1155 ⓦ www.leipzig-halle-airport.de

Lesser-known Altenburg Airport is 45 km (28 miles) from Leipzig and served by no-frills airline Ryanair, flying daily to London Stansted. A shuttle bus links the airport to Leipzig and takes roughly 1 hour and 15 minutes. ⓐ Altenburg Airport 1 ⓘ 0344 75 900 ⓦ www.flughafen-altenburg.de

By rail

It's a pleasure to pull into the immense Leipzig Hauptbahnhof, the city's main station. ICE trains operate an hourly service to major cities like Berlin (2–3 hours), Frankfurt (4 hours), Munich (7 hours) and Hamburg (4 hours 30 minutes). There are also direct connections to Dresden, Halle, Magdeburg, Dessau and Wittenberg.

A whopping €400 million has created a state-of-the-art travel and shopping experience at the station, which plays host to 140 shops, numerous cafés and restaurants and even a hair salon. Left luggage is located at exit 2 beneath platform 17. There's an information desk to help with timetables and bookings. ⓐ Willy-Brandt-Platz ⓦ www.bahnhof.de

◑ All aboard for a ride round Leipzig

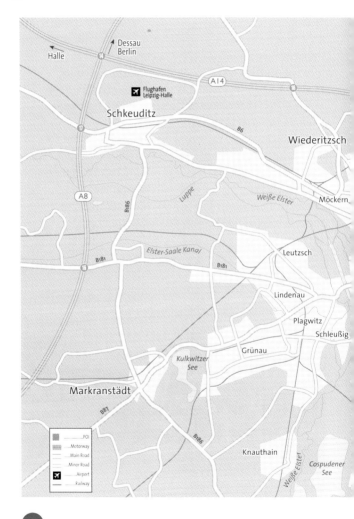

Around Leipzig

0   2 kilometres

0   1 mile

Leipzig Messe

Mockau

Taucha

Gohlis

Parthe

Schönefeld

Leipzig Station
Hauptbahnhof

B6

Borsdorf

LEIPZIG

Engelsdorf

Südvorstadt

Thonberg

Mölkau

A14

Stötteritz

B86

Völkerschlachtdenkmal

Holzhausen

Connewitz

Probstheida

Parthe

Markkleeberg

Markkleeberger
See

Großpösna

N

By bus

The bus station is in front of the Central Station. Eurolines and National Express serve a number of national and international destinations. Leipzig's public transport network, Leipziger Verkehrsbetriebe, operates a long-distance bus service to German cities including Berlin. Ⓦ www.lvb.de

By car

Leipzig is well connected to Germany and the rest of Europe via the A9 (Berlin–Leipzig–Nuremberg–Munich) and A14 (Magdeburg–Leipzig–Dresden) motorways. The ring road that encircles Leipzig has 14 motorway junctions: follow the signs for Leipzig–Mitte to reach the centre.

Driving is hassle-free and parking affordable in Leipzig. The easiest option is to park in the main station's huge multistorey car park, but make sure you have the right change as the ticket machine does not accept card payments.

FINDING YOUR FEET

Leipzig's residents are a friendly, easy-going and open-minded bunch, with a lively student population. The multicultural mix means that most of the locals, especially the younger generation, speak good English and are happy to help travellers out.

Leipzig is at the centre of Saxony's economic boom but, despite extraordinary growth, prices here have remained low. Leipzig was officially rated Europe's cheapest city in 2006.

Leipzig is generally a safe city with a low crime rate, but it's always wise to exert some caution, particularly if walking in dimly lit, less-populated areas at night.

ORIENTATION

Split in two by the White Elster River and fringed by floodplain forest, Leipzig is situated in the northwestern corner of Saxony in eastern Germany.

GETTING AROUND

On foot

As most attractions cluster in the compact and largely pedestrianised centre, walking is often the quickest, easiest and cheapest way to explore. Pick up a free map from the tourist office.

By bike

Leipzig has 200 km (125 miles) of marked bike trails to explore. You can hire your own set of wheels from Fahrradladen Eckhardt

IF YOU GET LOST, TRY ...

Excuse me, do you speak English?
Entschuldigen Sie, sprechen Sie Englisch?
Entshuldigen zee, shprekhen zee english?

Excuse me, is this the right way to the old town/the city centre/the tourist office/the station/the bus station?
Entschuldigung, geht es hier zur Altstadt/zur Stadtmitte/zur Touristeninformation/zum Bahnhof/zum Busbahnhof?
Entshuldeegoong, gayt es here tsoor altshtat/tsoor shtatmitter/zur Touristeninformasion/tsoom baanhof/tsoom busbaanhof?

Can you point to it on my map?
Können Sie es mir bitte auf der Karte zeigen?
Kernen see es meer bitter owf der kaarte tsygen?

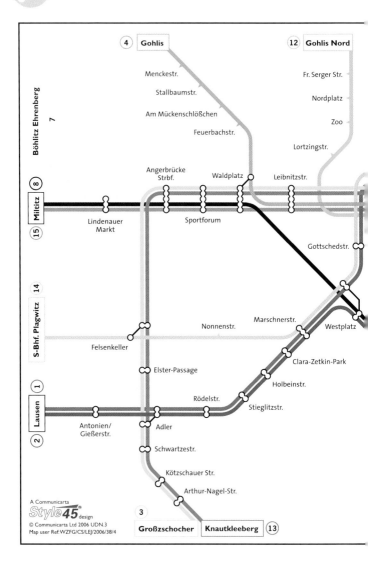

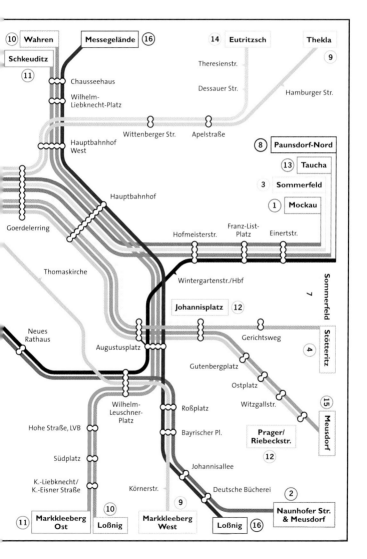

behind the main station. ⓐ Kurt-Schumacher-Strasse 4 ① 0341 961 7274 ⓦ www.bikeandsport.info

By tram

An extensive tram network criss-crosses the city. Make sure you validate your ticket at the stamping machine when boarding. If you're planning several trips, save with a day ticket for unlimited travel on public transport with Leipziger Verkehrsbetriebe (LVB).

By bus

Leipzig has 30 bus lines. It's worth investing in a 1- to 3-day Leipzig Welcome Card, which offers free travel on buses and trams, as well as discounts on the city's key attractions. It is available at a range of outlets including the Leipzig Information Centre, travel agents and many hotels, or online at www.leipzig.de/int/en/tourist/leipzig_card. Bus 89 is the city bus covering the centre's key attractions.

Car hire

Avis ⓐ Willy-Brandt-Platz 5 ① 0341 961 1400 ⓦ www.avis.com
Budget ⓐ Terminal 1 at Leipzig-Halle ① 0341 2241 880 ① 0341 2241 801 ⓦ www.europcar.com
Hertz ⓐ Terminal 1 at Leipzig-Halle ① 034204 14317 ① 034204 14390 ⓦ www.hertz.com
Europcar ⓐ Eutritzscher Strasse 24 ① 0341 904440 ① 0341 9044466 ⓦ www.europcar.com

● *Augustusplatz displays Leipzig's modern edge*

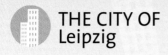

The City Centre

Mix jewel-box baroque buildings, cobbled inner courtyards and lofty Gothic churches with old-world arcades, pulsating nightlife and glass-fronted art galleries. Add a dash of Bach, a smidgen of Goethe, and there you have it: Leipzig city centre, a head-spinning cocktail of culture and contradictions.

SIGHTS & ATTRACTIONS

Ägyptisches Museum (Egyptology Museum)
Uncover mummies, funerary carvings and reliefs at this intriguing museum, part of the University of Leipzig.
ⓐ Burgstrasse 21 ⓣ 0341 973 7010 ⓦ www.uni-leipzig.de
ⓛ 13.00–17.00 Tues–Sat, 10.00–13.00 Sun, closed Mon; admission charge ⓣ Tram: 4, 7

Alte Handelsbörse (Old Stock Exchange)
Goethe's statue rises like a vision in front of this baroque edifice festooned with cherubs, golden garlands and coats of arms, the centrepiece of the cobbled Naschmarkt Square.
ⓐ Naschmarkt ⓣ 0341 261 7766 ⓣ Bus: 89

Altes Rathaus (Old Town Hall)
The cream-and-terracotta Renaissance town hall dominating the market square is one of Germany's most beautiful, featuring a domed clock tower and arcades. Behind the sturdy walls, you'll find the Stadtgeschichtliches Museum.
ⓐ Markt 1 ⓣ 0341 965 1320 ⓦ www.stadtgeschichtliches-

museum-leipzig.de 🕐 10.00–18.00 Tues–Sun, closed Mon; admission charge Ⓝ Bus: 89

Bach Museum

Set in the lemon-and-white Bosehaus, this museum traces the life of the city's most famous resident, Johann Sebastian Bach, with a superb collection of instruments and manuscripts.
ⓐ Thomaskirchhof 15–16 ☎ 0341 913 70 🌐 www.bach-leipzig.de
🕐 10.00–17.00 Mon–Sun; admission charge Ⓝ Tram: 9

Neue Rathaus (New Town Hall)

With its stone arches and silvery turrets, this vast neo-Renaissance town hall marks the spot where medieval

● The attractive Altes Rathaus is home to the State History Museum

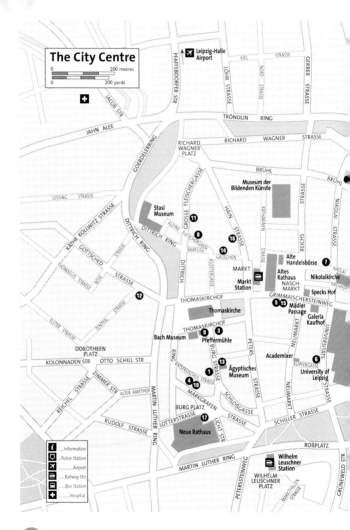

The City Centre

0 — 200 metres
0 — 200 yards

Leipzig-Halle Airport

Museum der Bildenden Künste

Stasi Museum

Alte Handelsbörse

Nikolaikirche

Altes Rathaus

Specks Hof

Mädler Passage

Galeria Kaufhof

Thomaskirche

Academixer

University of Leipzig

Bach Museum

Pfeffermühle

Ägyptisches Museum

Neue Rathaus

Wilhelm Leuschner Station

Information
Police Station
Airport
Railway Stn
Bus Station
Hospital

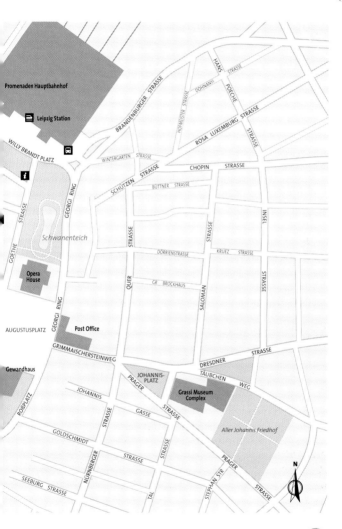

Pleissenburg castle once stood. Climb up for sweeping views over Leipzig's rooftops.

ⓐ Martin-Luther-Ring 4 ⓣ 0341 1230 ⓛ 10.00–18.00 Tues & Thur–Sun, 12.00–20.00 Wed, closed Mon; admission charge

ⓝ Tram: 9

Nikolaikirche (St Nicholas's Church)

Part Romanesque, part Gothic, this is where the 1989 Monday demonstrations took place that ultimately led to the reunification of Germany.

ⓐ Nikolaikirchhof 3 ⓣ 0341 960 5270 ⓦ www.nikolaikirche-leipzig.de ⓝ Bus: 89

● *The home of the famous boys' choir: Thomaskirche*

Thomaskirche (St Thomas's Church)

Bach worked as cantor for 27 years at this 13th-century church, where he now rests. Admire the cross-ribbed vaulting, Gothic nave, and marble-and-alabaster baptismal font. It's still home to the renowned St Thomas's Boys Choir – come at the weekend to hear them perform.

ⓐ Thomaskirchhof 18 ⓣ 0341 960 2855
ⓦ www.thomaskirche.org ⓔ thomaskirche.leipzig@t-online.de
ⓛ 09.00–18.00 Mon–Sun ⓝ Tram: 9

University of Leipzig

Founded in 1409, the University of Leipzig is one of Germany's oldest centres of academic excellence; this building dates back to 1974.

ⓐ Universitäts Strasse/Augustusplatz ⓦ www.uni-leipzig.de
ⓝ Tram: 7, 10, 13, 15

CULTURE

Academixer

If you speak some German, it is well worth catching a performance at this satirical cabaret and comedy venue.

ⓐ Kupfergasse ⓣ 0341 2178 7878 ⓦ www.academixer.com
ⓔ info@academixer.com ⓝ Tram: 10, 11

Gewandhaus

The Gewandhaus Orchestra takes the stage at this glass-walled concert hall on Augustusplatz. In the foyer, see Europe's biggest ceiling fresco, Sighard Gille's *Song of Life*.

ⓐ Augustusplatz 8 ☎ 0341 12700 ⓦ www.gewandhaus.de
ⓔ ticket@gewandhaus.de ⏰ (Box office) 10.00–18.00 Mon–Fri,
10.00–14.00 Sat, closed Sun Ⓝ Tram: 7, 10, 13, 15

Grassi Museum Complex

Displays range from arts and crafts via Renaissance lutes to
African artefacts in this trio of museums.
ⓐ Johannisplatz 5–11 ☎ 0341 973 1973 ⓦ www.grassimuseum.de
⏰ 10.00–18.00 Tues–Sun, closed Mon; admission charge
Ⓝ Tram: 4, 7, 12, 15

Museum der Bildenden Künste – MDBK (Fine Arts Museum)

This crystalline cube reflects Michael Fischer-Art's work covering
the buildings opposite. Seek out Max Klinger's striking
Beethoven sculpture (1885), shaped from marble, alabaster and
bronze. Other highlights include works by Dutch Masters and
Impressionists, plus Ecker's oversized red whistles.
ⓐ Katherinen Strasse 10 ☎ 0341 216 990 ⓦ www.mdbk.de
⏰ 10.00–18.00 Tues & Thur–Sun, 12.00–20.00 Wed, closed Mon;
admission charge

Opera House

Illuminated by night, Leipzig's opera house on Augustusplatz
opened in 1960 on the site of the New Theatre which was
bombed during World War II. The repertoire ranges from opera
and musicals to cutting-edge ballet.
ⓐ Augustusplatz 12 ☎ 0341 126 1261 ⓦ www.oper-leipzig.de
ⓔ service@oper-leipzig.de ⏰ (Box office) 08.00–20.00 Mon–Fri,
10.00–16.00 Sat Ⓝ Tram: 7, 10, 13, 15

Pfeffermühle

Satirical cabaret in the courtyard is the appeal of this atmospheric bar and comedy club, housed in the baroque Bosehaus.
ⓐ Thomaskirchhof 16 ⓣ 0341 960 3196 ⓦ www.Kabarett-Leipziger-Pfeffermuehle.de ⓛ 18.00–open end Mon–Sun
ⓝ Tram: 9

Stasi Museum

Home to Leipzig's Stasi (secret police) headquarters until 1989, this round-cornered building offers a fascinating insight into Leipzig's troubled past.
ⓐ Dittrich Ring 24 ⓣ 0341 961 2443 ⓦ www.runde-ecke-leipzig.de ⓛ 10.00–18.00 Mon–Sun ⓝ Tram: 3, 7, 15

RETAIL THERAPY

Bodo Zeidler This dinky boutique is one of the best places to shop for blue-and-white Meissener porcelain. ⓐ Markt 1 ⓣ 0341 960 1714 ⓦ www.bodo-zeidler.de ⓛ 10.00–19.00 Mon–Fri, 10.00–16.00 Sat, closed Sun ⓝ Bus: 89

Der Liebesladen Pick up engagement, wedding and anniversary gifts at this love-struck shop opposite Thomaskirche.
ⓐ Thomaskirchhof 11 ⓣ 0341 215 5976 ⓦ www.polterbehr.de
ⓛ 12.00–18.30 Mon–Fri, 10.00–13.00 Sat, closed Sun ⓝ Tram: 9

Galeria Kaufhof Find everything under one roof at this department store giant. ⓐ Neumarkt 1 ⓣ 0341 22 450 ⓦ www.galeria-kaufhof.de ⓛ 09.30–20.00 Mon–Sat, closed Sun ⓝ Tram: 7, 10

Heidrich & Zeidler There's a year-round smell and feel of Christmas at this Lilliputian shop selling handmade matchbox toys, wooden pyramids and traditional Erzgebirge decorations. ⓐ Markt 1 ⓣ 0341 1248 347 ⓛ 10.00–19.00 Mon–Fri, 10.00–16.00 Sat, closed Sun ⓝ Bus: 89

La Barrica Spanish specialities from Manchego cheese to Rioja wines share shelf space at this hole-in-the-wall gourmet shop opposite St Nicholas's Church. It's a good place to stock up on tapas for a picnic. ⓐ Ritterstrasse 4 ⓣ 0341 961 4334

⬥ *Glass and glamour in the Promenaden Hauptbahnhof*

ⓦ www.labarrica-albrecht.de ⓛ 12.00–20.00 Mon-Fri, 11.00–16.00 Sat, closed Sun ⓝ Bus: 89

Mädler Passage Whether you're seeking twinkling Swarovski crystals or Armani originals, the sleek boutiques lining Leipzig's most elegant arcade come up with the goods. This is also a pleasant spot to rest your feet and enjoy a light lunch or coffee. ⓐ Mädler Passage ⓣ 0341 216 340 ⓦ www.maedler-passage-leipzig.de ⓝ Bus: 89

Petersbogen Opposite the New Town Hall, this modern glass mall houses a cinema and casino, plus a string of shops. ⓐ Peters Strasse 36–44 ⓣ 0341 217 1785 ⓦ www.petersbogen.com ⓝ Tram: 9

Promenaden Hauptbahnhof The main station's gleaming mall shelters 80 shops that stay open late, stocking everything from fashion to fresh flowers and fine wines. ⓐ Willy-Brandt-Platz 7 ⓣ 0341 141 270 ⓦ www.promenaden-hauptbahnhof-leipzig.de ⓛ 09.30–22.00 Mon–Sat, closed Sun ⓝ Train: main station

Schmuckwerk Accessorise with beads and bangles from this arty jeweller, displaying quirky creations by Leipzig designers ⓐ Naschmarkt ⓣ 0341 961 5278 ⓦ www.schmuckwerk.de ⓛ 11.00–19.30 Mon–Fri, 11.00–18.00 Sat, closed Sun ⓝ Bus: 89

Specks Hof Murals, courtyards and narrow passages define Leipzig's oldest arcade, the place to come for designer wear and original art. ⓐ Reichs Strasse 4–6 ⓝ Tram: 7, 10

TAKING A BREAK

Aladdin £ ❶ The pick of the budget bunch, this haunt serves tasty Turkish snacks – €5 is enough for quite a feast. Save some room for sticky baklava and almond-stuffed pistachio balls.
ⓐ Burg Strasse 12 ⓣ 0170 97 66 707 Ⓝ Tram: 9

Bagel Brothers £ ❷ A café by day and funky bar by night, fill up here on fresh bagels, chicken fajitas and frozen yoghurts. In summer, the terrace transforms into a beach complete with paddling pool and palms. ⓐ Nikolai Strasse 42 ⓣ 0341 980 3330
Ⓦ www.bagelbrothers.com Ⓛ 06.30–23.30 Mon–Thur, 06.30–02.00 Fri, 07.30–02.00 Sat, 08.30–23.30 Sun
Ⓝ Train: main station

Café Kandler £ ❸ Sample teas named after Bach, Wagner and Mozart, with Leipziger Lerche cakes or Bachtaler pralines.
ⓐ Thomaskirchhof 11 ⓣ 0341 213 2181 Ⓝ Tram: 9

Gelateria Palazzese £ ❹ Savour handmade basil, poppy and marzipan ice creams on the terrace of this cave-like parlour.
ⓐ Ratsfreischul Strasse 6–8 ⓣ 0341 962 9975 Ⓦ www.grotta-palazzese.de Ⓛ 11.00–23.30 Mon–Sun Ⓝ Tram: 9

Kümmel Apotheke £ ❺ Divas grace the walls at this wood-floored bistro, where locals sip coffee and *kümmel* (caraway seed) liqueur. ⓐ Mädler Passage ⓣ 0341 960 8705
Ⓦ www.kuemmel-apotheke.de ⓔ info@kuemmel-apotheke.de
Ⓛ 09.30–01.00 Mon–Sat, 10.30–21.00 Sun Ⓝ Tram: 9

Mokkaflip £ ❻ Next to the university, this student hangout oozes retro cool. Sink into a leather sofa to try a tiger spice latte or green tortoise tea. Free WiFi access is available. ⓐ Universitätsstrasse 16 ❶ 0341 999 9555 ⓦ www.mokkaflip.de ⓛ 09.00–20.00 Mon–Fri, 10.00–20.00 Sat, 11.00–20.00 Sun ⓝ Tram: 7, 10, 13, 15

Riquet £ ❼ Elephant heads guard the door at this Viennese-style café, with its dark polished wood and sweeping staircase. ⓐ Schumachergäschen 1 ❶ 0341 961 0000 ⓦ www.riquethaus.de ⓔ café@riquethaus.de ⓛ 09.00–22.00 Sun–Thur, 09.00–24.00 Fri–Sat, closed Sun ⓝ Bus: 89

Zum Arabischen Coffe Baum ££ ❽ A Leipzig institution dating back to 1720, Europe's oldest coffee shop houses three cafés, three à la carte restaurants and a caffeine-inspired museum. ⓐ Kleine Fleischergasse 4 ❶ 0341 961 0060 ⓦ www.coffe-baum.de ⓝ Tram: 9

AFTER DARK

Restaurants
Central Apotheke £ ❾ If you need a cure for hunger, Leipzig's first homeopath is just the ticket. Eat *Leipziger Allerlei* stew and drink Gose beer on the terrace facing St Thomas's Church. ⓐ Thomaskirchhof Square 12 ❶ 0341 211 8299 ⓛ 11.00–24.00 Mon–Sun ⓝ Tram: 9

Grotta Palazzese £ ❿ Feast on fresh fish beside stalactites and stalagmites in this Italian bistro designed like a cave.

ⓐ Ratsfreischulstrasse 6–8 ⓣ 0341 962 9974 ⓦ www.grotta-palazzese.de ⓛ 11.30–14.30, 17.30–23.30 Mon–Sun ⓝ Tram: 9

Mr Moto £ ⑪ Minimalist design characterises this trendy sushi bar. Watch your spicy prawns and sake salmon drift past on little boats. ⓐ Grosse Fleischergasse 21 ⓣ 0341 212 7898 ⓛ 12.00–14.00, 16.30–01.00 Mon–Fri, 12.00–01.00 Sat, 16.00–01.00 Sun ⓝ Tram: 12

Sol y Mar £ ⑫ Eat lying down in this ultra-sleek restaurant. Cream drapes, plush cushions and Balinese furniture create a relaxed mood, and you can even have a massage before dinner. ⓐ Gottsched Strasse 4 ⓣ 0341 961 5721 ⓦ www.sol-y-mar.net ⓛ 09.00–open end Mon–Sun ⓝ Tram: 14

Thüringerhof £ ⑬ Martin Luther and Schumann once frequented this 500-year-old restaurant, where you can dine on *Eisbein* (pickled pork with sauerkraut) beneath a vaulted ceiling. ⓐ Burg Strasse 19 ⓣ 0341 994 4999 ⓦ www.thueringer-hof.de ⓔ reservierung@theuringer-hof.de ⓛ 11.00–24.00 Mon–Sun ⓝ Tram: 9

Varadero £ ⑭ Shark steaks and garlicky *gambas* land on your plate in this funky Cuban restaurant. ⓐ Barfussgässchen 8 ⓣ 0341 960 09 26 ⓛ 11.30–open end Mon–Sun ⓝ Bus: 89

Auerbachs Keller ££ ⑮ This cavernous 16th-century cellar, Leipzig's most famous restaurant, was a favourite haunt of Goethe who penned *Faust* here. Tuck into *Tafelspitz* (braised

beef) with potato dumplings. ⓐ Mädler Passage ① 0341 216 100
ⓦ www.auerbachs-keller-leipzig.de ⓔ info@auerbachs-keller-
leipzig.de ① 11.30–24.00 Mon–Sun ⓝ Bus: 89

Barthels Hof ££ ⑯ Sample spit-roasted pork and salted
herrings in this 500-year-old restaurant's inner courtyard.
ⓐ Hain Strasse 1 ① 0341 141 310 ⓦ www.barthels-hof.de
① 07.00–24.00 Mon–Sun ⓝ Bus: 89

Ratskeller ££ ⑰ Vaulted ceilings and stone arches set the
scene in this art nouveau restaurant. ⓐ Lotterstrasse 1 ① 0341
123 4567 ⓦ www.ratskeller-leipzig.de ⓔ info@ratskeller-
leipzig.de ① 11.00–23.00 Mon–Sat, 11.00–15.30 Sun
ⓝ Tram: 9

DRALLEWATSCH

Saxon slang for pub-crawl, the *Drallewatsch* centres around
the bustling Barfussgässchen and Fleischergasse, where wall-
to-wall bars, clubs, restaurants and open-air cafés vie for your
attention. Things heat up about midnight when Leipzig's
party people brace themselves for a big night out with
cocktails on the terrace – try Bellini's or the Zebra Bar – before
moving onto a live concert in Spizz or Bar Fusz. Next up are
clubs like Pflaumenbaum, Roxy and Alpen Max where revellers
dance to everything from Russian disco to R'n'B grooves. The
good news for night-owls is that most places on the bar mile
have 24-hour licensing, referred to locally as 'open end', which
means that the fun only stops when your feet do!

Bars & clubs

Alpen Max Full of scantily-clad staff, hens and stags, this raucous club is dubbed Saxony's biggest ski chalet. ⓐ Grosse Fleischergasse 12 ⓣ 0341 962 86 24 ⓦ www.discofun.de
ⓛ 21.00–open end Mon, Thur, Fri & Sat, closed Tues, Wed & Sun
ⓝ Tram: 12

Bar Fusz Bursting at the seams at weekends, this bar is hot, loud and happening. Partygoers spill out onto the heated terrace. Catch live bands here on a Saturday night. ⓐ Barfussgässchen 6
ⓣ 0341 962 8624 ⓛ 12.00–open end Mon–Sun ⓝ Bus: 89

Bellini's Smooth funk plays as you sip a blackberry margarita in this lively cocktail bar, decked out with black-and-white pictures of jazz legends. ⓐ Barfussgässchen 3 ⓣ 0341 9617 681
ⓛ 12.00–open end Mon–Sun ⓝ Bus: 89

Kildare If you've got a craving for Guinness, fish 'n' chips and big-screen sports, this cheery Irish pub hits the spot.
ⓐ Barfussgässchen 3–7 ⓣ 0341 983 9740 ⓛ 12.00–open end Mon–Sun ⓝ Bus: 89

Mephisto Sway to live jazz and sip cocktails at this Goethe-inspired bar. Look into the mirror to hear the devilish Mephisto cackle. ⓐ Mädler Passage ⓣ 0341 216 100 ⓛ 11.00–02.00 Mon–Sat closed Sun ⓝ Bus: 89

Moritzbastei Part of the old city walls, this chilled student club is set in a huge red-brick building around a central courtyard.

There's always something bubbling – from open-air jam sessions to club nights. ⓐ Universitäts Strasse 9 ⓣ 0341 702 590 ⓦ www.moritzbastei.de ⓛ 10.00–open end Mon–Fri, 12.00–open end Sat, 09.00–open end Sun ⓝ Tram: 7, 10, 13, 15

Spizz Jazz & Music Club Young trendies drink mango daiquiris on this buzzy bar's terrace. In the basement, the Jazz Keller stages live blues and jazz, plus DJs pumping out soul and R'n'B. ⓐ Markt 9 ⓣ 0341 960 8043 ⓦ www.spizz.org ⓛ 09.00–open end Mon–Sun ⓝ Bus: 89

Zebra Bar This safari-themed bar serving cool caipirinhas will have you seeing spots and stripes. ⓐ Barfussgässchen 2 ⓣ 0341 149 4990 ⓛ 20.00–open end ⓝ Bus: 89

Zur Pleissenburg Blink and you'll miss this quirky low-ceilinged watering hole full of local flavour. ⓐ Ratsfreischulstrasse 2 ⓣ 0341 960 2653 ⓛ 09.00–05.00 Mon–Sun ⓝ Tram: 9

● *Have a devilish time at Mephisto*

Plagwitz & Südvorstadt

A stark contrast to the north's art nouveau and the centre's baroque grandeur, Leipzig's sassy south has urban edge and a boho vibe. The cogs and wheels of this once industrial area have been turned towards modern art and cutting-edge culture, transforming red-brick factories into galleries, chichi restaurants and buzzy bars.

SIGHTS & ATTRACTIONS

Asisi Factory Panometer

The brainchild of artist Yadegar Asisi, this striking gallery reels in the crowds with life-sized 360-degree panoramas from Mount Everest to Ancient Rome. Originally a gasometer, the sphere-shaped, red-bricked space has been given a new lease of life as a 'panometer'.

📍 R. Lehmann Strasse 📞 0341 121 3396 🌐 www.asisi-factory.de 🕐 09.00–19.00 Tues–Fri, 10.00–20.00 Sat & Sun; admission charge 🚊 Tram: 90, Bus: 70

Botanischen Garten (Botanical Gardens)

Neat and petite, the University of Leipzig's botanical gardens are Germany's oldest, dating back to 1542. Wander the themed gardens to spot species like European orchids and the South American *Gunnera chilensis*, resembling a giant rhubarb. The greenhouses nurture cacti, ferns and 200 butterfly varieties.

📍 Linné Strasse 1 📞 0341 973 6850 🌐 www.uni-leipzig.de 🕐 09.00–20.00 (summer), 09.00–16.00 (winter) 🚊 Tram: 2, 21

Bundesverwaltungsgericht (Federal Administrative Court)

While a court may not top your sightseeing list, it's worth making an effort to see this one. This grand neo-Renaissance edifice overshadows Simsonplatz, with its soaring columns, domes and sculpted lions. Take a peek inside to glimpse the frescoed ballroom.

ⓐ Simsonplatz 1 ❶ 0341 200 70 ⓦ www.bverwg.de
🕐 08.00–16.00 Mon-Fri, closed Sat & Sun Ⓝ Tram: 9

Clara-Zetkin-Park

Sliced in two by the White Elster River, this expansive park to the southwest of the centre is an oasis of calm. Thick canopies of plane and beech trees provide welcome shade on hot days. Relax beside the fountains and roses in the pretty Palmengarten.

❶ 0341 123 6099 Ⓝ Tram: 1, 2

Museum für Druckkunst (Museum of Printing Art)

Trace Leipzig's centuries-old printing history at this hands-on museum in Plagwitz, housed in a red-brick factory. Interactive displays give an insight into publishing industry techniques.

ⓐ Nonnen Strasse 38 ❶ 0341 231 620 ⓦ www.druckkunst-museum.de 🕐 10.00–17.00 Mon–Fri, 11.00–17.00 Sun, closed Sat; admission charge Ⓝ Tram: 1, 2

Rübesams Da Capo

Check out this vintage car museum (look out for the Interflug plane on the roof), where old-timers gleam against the backdrop of a beautifully restored red-brick factory.

ⓐ Karl-Heine-Strasse 105 ❶ 0341 926 0137

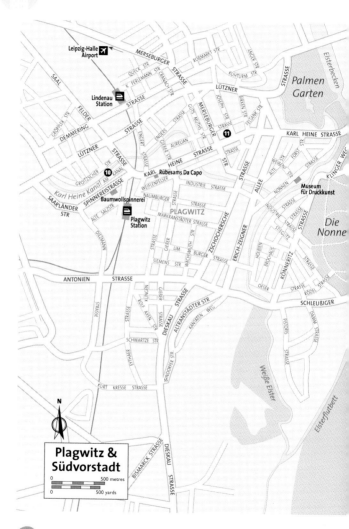

Plagwitz & Südvorstadt

0   500 metres
0   500 yards

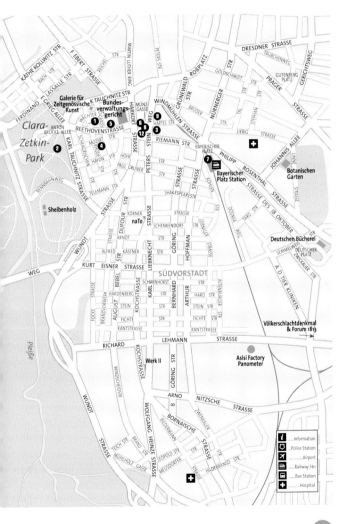

www.ruebesam-dacapo.de 11.00–18.00 Tues–Sat,
10.00–18.00 Sun, closed Mon; admission charge Tram: 14

Scheibenholz

Place a bet at this 140-year-old horse-racing track, Leipzig's
oldest sports venue. Bordering Clara-Zetkin-Park, this venue is
open during the racing season (May to October).
Rennbahnweg 2 0341 960 4327 www.galopprennbahn-
scheibenholz.de mail@galopprennbahn-scheibenholz.de
Bus: 89

Völkerschlachtdenkmal (Monument to the Battle of Nations)

Soaring above Leipzig, this grey monolith was built to
commemorate the 100th anniversary of the Battle of the
Nations against Napoleon's troops. Guarded by a statue of
St Michael, the 96-m (315-ft) high memorial's viewing platform
affords far-reaching views over Leipzig. Both the huge stone
sculptures and the climb to the top are breathtaking.
Prager Strasse 0341 878 0471
www.voelkerschlachtdenkmal.de 10.00–18.00 (summer),
10.00–16.00 (winter); admission charge Tram: 2, 15

CULTURE

Baumwollspinnerei

Housed in a former cotton mill, this labyrinthine venue
comprises a string of cavernous halls staging events from
improvised theatre to jazz concerts. The galleries showcase
works by local and international artists.

@ Spinnereistrasse 7 ❶ 0341 498 0270 Ⓦ www.spinnerei.de
@ mail@spinnerei.de Ⓝ Tram: 14

Deutschen Bücherei (German National Library)

Dominating Deutscher Platz, this huge building is festooned with portraits of Goethe and Gutenberg. The German Book and Script Museum explores script and printing techniques.
@ Deutscher Platz 1 ❶ 0341 2271 324 Ⓦ www.ddb.de @ dbsm@
dbl.ddb.de ❶ 09.00–16.00 Mon–Sat, closed Sun Ⓝ Tram: 16

Forum 1813

Next to the Monument to the Battle of the Nations, this museum recounts the historic events leading up to the battle in 1813. You'll need an extra ticket to see the 350 objects on display,

🔺 *Get in a spin at this old cotton mill, Baumwollspinnerei*

which include a model of Leipzig on a scale of 1:72. Some explanations are given in English.

ⓐ Prager Strasse ⓣ 0341 878 0471

ⓦ www.voelkerschlachtdenkmal.de ⓛ 10.00–18.00 (summer), 10.00–16.00 (winter); admission charge ⓝ Tram: 2, 15

Galerie für Zeitgenössische Kunst (Contemporary Art Gallery)

Avant-garde art graces the stark white walls at this multimedia gallery, sheltering contemporary paintings, photography and sculpture. Most of the permanent collection dates back to Leipzig's GDR times.

ⓐ Karl-Tauchnitz-Strasse 11 ⓣ 0341 140 810 ⓦ www.gfzk.de

ⓔ office@gfzk.de ⓛ 14.00–19.00 Tues–Sat, 12.00–19.00 Sun

ⓝ Tram: 2, 8

naTo

Film, theatre, literature, politics and music push the boundaries of convention at this arts centre. The offerings range from experimental jazz to Tibetan overtone singing, but the venue also stages fun summer events like the bathtub race and soapbox derby.

ⓐ Karl-Liebknecht-Strasse 46 ⓣ 0341 301 4397 ⓦ www.nato-leipzig.de ⓔ info@nato-leipzig.de ⓝ Tram: 10, 11

Werk II

Catch alternative cultural events at this former gasometer, a 19th-century red-and-sand brick building.

ⓐ Kochstrasse 132 ⓣ 0341 308 0140 ⓦ www.werk-2.de

ⓔ info@werk-2.de ⓝ Tram: 9, 10, 11

TAKING A BREAK

Coffito £ ❶ When hunger strikes, refuel at this café serving freshly pressed juices and filling wraps. Ⓐ Ferdinand-Rhode-Strasse 3b ❶ 0341 225 4823 ❶ 09.00–18.00 Mon–Sun
Ⓝ Bus: 89

Glashaus £ ❷ Surrounded by greenery, this café is the perfect spot to put your feet up after a long stroll in Clara-Zetkin-Park. Take a pew in the leafy beer garden or conservatory to enjoy a cappuccino, beer or ice cream. The restaurant is wheelchair accessible. Ⓐ Clara-Zetkin-Park ❶ 0341 9 62 7873 ❶ 09.00–23.00 (summer), 10.00–23.00 (autumn) Ⓝ Tram: 1

Grüne Tomaten £ ❸ Crammed with memorabilia from the cult film *Fried Green Tomatoes*, this weird and wonderful café is a find. The rustic décor has unusual touches such as an HMV gramophone, velvet cushions and baskets suspended from the ceiling. Ⓐ Härtel Strasse 27 ❶ 0341 583 2548 Ⓦ www. gruene-tomate-leipzig.de ❶ 09.00–20.00 Mon, Tues & Thur, 09.00–24.00 Wed & Fri, 16.00–24.00 Sat, closed Sun
Ⓝ Tram: 10, 11

Kowalski Café £ ❹ Arty types and music students hang out in this laid-back, bistro-style café glammed up with a dark wood floor and deep red walls. The counter is full of tempting cakes, which you can savour with a coffee on the terrace.
Ⓐ Ferdinand-Rhode-Strasse 12 ❶ 0341 212 6020 ❶ 09.00–01.00 Mon–Fri, 09.00–02.00 Sat Ⓝ Bus: 89

Studentenwerk Leipzig £ **⑤** This relaxed university café opposite the Albertina Library sells fair-trade coffee and snacks for next to nothing. Join the students on the terrace in summer. ⓐ Beethovenstrasse ⓦ www.studentenwerk-leipzig.de ⓛ 08.00–20.00 Mon–Thur, 08.00–19.00 Fri, closed Sat & Sun ⓝ Tram: 9

Suppa Sumarum £ **⑥** Relax on the cushion-lined benches to study the impressive soup menu at this café: choices range from flavoursome carrot and mandarin to spicy fish soup from Sierra Leone. If you're still peckish, munch on a feta, peach and strawberry salad, washed back with an apple-and-mint cocktail. ⓐ Münz Gasse 16 ⓣ 0341 149 4974 ⓦ www.suppe-leipzig.de ⓛ 11.30– 24.00 Mon–Fri, 17.00–24.00 Sat, closed Sun ⓝ Tram: 10, 11

AFTER DARK

Restaurants
Bayerischer Bahnhof £ **⑦** History seeps from every pore of this 19th-century former railway terminus. Today the brewery churns out litres of the famous Gose beer. Quench your thirst in the huge shaded beer garden, or feast on roast pork in ale beside shiny brass boilers in the wood-panelled restaurant. ⓐ Bayerischer Platz 1 ⓣ 0341 124 5760 ⓦ www.bayerischer-bahnhof.de ⓛ 11.00–open end Mon–Sun ⓝ Tram: 16

Beirut Night £ **⑧** Rich colours and Lebanese food tempt at this little restaurant on Münzgasse. Dishes like falafel (chickpea balls), halloumi (fried cheese) and honey-drenched baklava are

MESSING ABOUT ON THE RIVER

Nicknamed Little Venice, the river and canals flowing through Plagwitz reveal a different side to Leipzig. Explore the web of waterways by hiring a rowing boat or letting someone else do the hard work. The trip passes natural and industrial landscapes – look up to spy towering plane trees and lofty chimneys.

Those feeling active can rent canoes from the boathouse (Klingerweg 2) or join a three-hour rafting tour departing from Paulis Caféteria (Könneritzstrasse 14). If a lazy cruise sounds more appealing, head for Ristorante Da Vito (Nonnenstrasse 11), where the Italian owner has gone to the pains of importing real Venetian gondolas to shuttle passengers along the White Elster River. For more details, contact the tourist office.

ⓐ Richard-Wagner-Strasse 1 ⓣ 0341 7104-265
ⓦ www.leipzig.de ⓔ Info@LTS-Leipzig.de ⓛ 10.00–18.00 Mon–Fri, 09.00–16.00 Sat & Sun

🔺 *Cruising for pleasure on the White Elster River*

on the menu alongside a selection of water pipes – choose from rose, mango and peppermint. ⓐ Münz Gasse 7 ⓣ 0341 962 8288 ⓦ www.beirut-night.de ⓛ 16.00–24.00 Sat–Mon, 11.30–14.30, 16.00–24.00 Tues–Fri ⓝ Tram: 10, 11

China White £ ❾ This bright and airy restaurant offers flavoursome Chinese fare such as Peking soup, crispy duck and chop choi. ⓐ Peters Stein Weg 17 ⓣ 0341 149 1966 ⓔ chinawhite-leipzig@web.de ⓛ 11.30–14.30, 17.30–23.00 Mon–Sun ⓝ Tram: 10, 11

Kanal 28 £ ❿ This former tile factory has been resurrected as a funky restaurant, café and cultural centre. Overlooking the Karl-Heine Canal, the red-brick building attracts a boho crowd to its spacious terrace and art gallery. ⓐ Am Canal 28 ⓣ 0341 497 2430 ⓦ www.kanal-28.de ⓛ 15.00–open end Tues–Fri, 10.00–open end Sat & Sun, closed Mon ⓝ Tram: 14

Pinocchio £ ⓫ Specialities from south Tirol to Sicily whet appetites at this cheery Italian restaurant and pizzeria. When the weather warms, enjoy a glass of Chianti beneath the trees on the terrace. ⓐ Karl-Heine-Strasse 27 ⓣ 0341 480 3856 ⓦ www.pinocchio-leipzig.de ⓛ 11.30–24.00 (summer), 11.30–14.30, 18.00–24.00 Mon–Fri, 11.30–24.00 Sat & Sun (winter) ⓝ Tram: 1, 2

Piagor ££ ⓬ Mint-green tones, wood floors and a minimalist décor set the scene at this contemporary restaurant, where creative dishes with an emphasis on fresh fish include spicy papaya-melon soup with king prawns, Andalusian octopus and lobster ravioli. ⓐ Münz Gasse 3 ⓣ 0341 1494778 ⓦ www.piagor.de ⓛ 11.30–14.30 Mon–Fri & 18.00–01.00 Mon–Sun ⓝ Tram: 10, 11

Bars & clubs

Flower Power Love, peace and rock 'n' roll rule in this spit-and-sawdust pub. The colours are psychedelic, drinks cheap and vibe very mellow... ⓐ Riemann Strasse 42 ⓣ 0341 961 3441 ⓦ www.Flowerpower.eu ⓛ 19.00–open end Mon–Sun ⓝ Tram: 10, 11

Havana Hips sway to sultry Latino tunes at this Cuban club. DJs keep the dance floor packed playing salsa, merengue and cumbia rhythms. If you've got two left feet come early in the evening to take pointers from the experts at the dance classes. ⓐ Karl-Liebknecht-Strasse 10 ⓣ 0176 298 66329 ⓦ www.havana-leipzig.de ⓛ 20.00–open end Wed–Sat, closed Sun–Tues ⓝ Tram: 10, 11

Nova Barocca How often have you needed a stiff drink after getting your hair done? At this salon-cum-cocktail bar decked out in marvellously over-the-top baroque style, divas can get their hair cut, nails polished and back massaged before sipping wine and nibbling on exotic fruits. ⓐ Münz Gasse 22 ⓣ 0341 230 6620 ⓦ www.nova-barocca.de ⓛ 10.00–open end Tues–Sat ⓝ Tram: 10, 11

Reich & Schön Rich and beautiful is the name of this lounge-style nightspot in Südvorstadt's bar mile, where bright young things sip cocktails beside pastel-hued walls striped like candy canes. The big draw is the music, moving from R'n'B and smooth jazz to soul and funk. ❷ Münz Gasse 18 ❶ 0341 230 6158 ⏰ 19.00–open end Mon–Sat, closed Sun Ⓝ Tram: 10, 11

Stäv Put your beer goggles on to drink Cologne's favourite tipple, gold-hued Kölsch, at this relaxed pub doubling as a restaurant. The walls are smothered in photos of some of the luminaries and politicians that have shaped Leipzig's history since 1945. ❷ Peters Stein Weg 10 ❶ 0341 149 3366 ⓦ www.staev-leipzig.de ⏰ 11.00–open end Mon–Sat, 10.00–open end Sun Ⓝ Tram: 10, 11

Triangel This snug, unassuming pub might look like any other until you step inside and see the walls lined with board games instead of beer glasses – 600 to be precise. So if you fancy a quick game of *Bluff* or want to while away the hours over chess and cheap beer, this popular haunt is the place to come. ❷ Peter Stein Weg 10 ❶ 0341 149 7707 ⓦ www.triangel-le.de ⏰ 10.00–02.00 Mon–Sun Ⓝ Tram: 10, 11

Gohlis & Zoo

Greenery, Gose and goals drive most visitors to venture north of the centre. Culture and commerce have also made their mark here – grand merchant villas and stately art nouveau homes punctuate tree-lined boulevards, once home to wealthy merchants and fur traders.

SIGHTS & ATTRACTIONS

Aussichtsturm (Rosental Tower)

Rising above a canopy of trees, this 20-m (66-ft) tower crowns a hill in Rosental Park. It's a bit of a wobbly climb to the top, but the sweeping views over Leipzig's thick woodlands, canals and cityscape are well worth the effort.

ⓐ Rosental ⓦ www.leipzig-gohlis.de ⓝ Tram: 3, 7, 12, 16

Michaeliskirche (St Michael's Church)

Pinned to the centre of Nordplatz, this is one of Leipzig's true hidden gems. Blending neo-Renaissance, neo-Gothic and art nouveau styles, the church captivates with its silver-grey domes, a huge octagonal tower and sublime marble altar.

ⓐ Nordplatz 14 ⓣ 0341 54 5509 ⓦ www.michaelis-friedens.de
ⓝ Tram: 12

Nordplatz

Admire the tall art nouveau townhouses framing this peaceful square or relax beside the roses in the tiny, tree-lined park. Look up to see the bell tower topping the

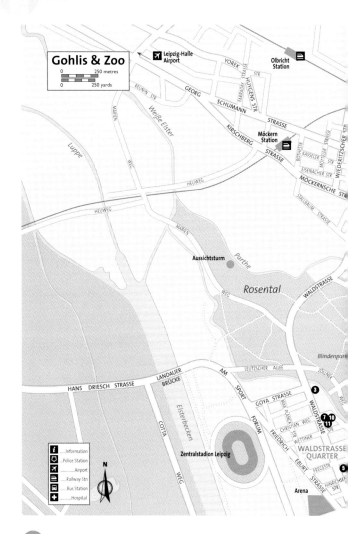

Gohlis & Zoo

| 0 | 250 metres |
| 0 | 250 yards |

Leipzig-Halle Airport

Olbricht Station

YOREK STR

FARADAY STR

TESLA STR

HUYGENS STR

REUNIN STR

GEORG

SCHUMANN

STRASSE

MAREN

Weiße Elster

KIRSCHBERG

Möckern Station

BOTHESTR

KASSELER STR

MITTLER STR

WIEDERITZSCHER STR

STRASSE

Luppe

HEUWEG

EISENACHER STR

MÖCKERNSCHE STR

STALLBAUM STRASSE

HEUWEG

MAREN

Parthe

Aussichtsturm

Rosental

WEG

WALDSTRASSE

Blindenpark

ZÖLLNE

LANDAUER BRÜCKE

AM

LEUTZSCHER ALLEE

HANS DRIESCH STRASSE

SPORT

GOYA STRASSE

MAX PLANCK WEG

3

CHRISTIAN WEG

WALDSTRASSE

Elsterbecken

FORUM

WETTINER

7 10

11

COTTA

FRIEDRICH

WALDSTRASSE
QUARTER

EBURT

Zentralstadion Leipzig

TRECESTR

5

WEG

Arena

STRASSE

HINRICHSEN STR

i	Information
	Police Station
✈	Airport
	Railway Stn
	Bus Station
✚	Hospital

N

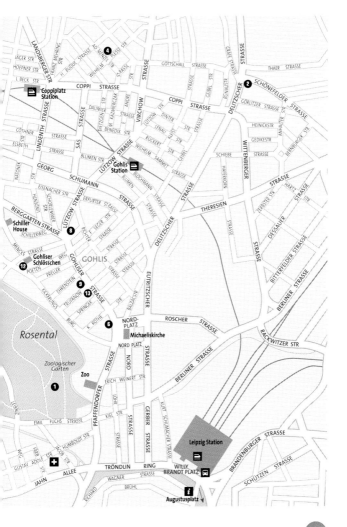

cream-and-terracotta Leibnizschule Gymnasium school, a
striking turn-of-the-century building.
 www.leipzig-gohlis.de Ⓝ Tram: 12

Rosental Park

The green lungs of Leipzig, this is an expansive pocket of
greenery northwest of the centre. Pathways weave through
untamed woodlands and heath on one side and English-style
gardens on the other; the park is so big it never feels crowded. Be
sure to visit the Blindenpark, a garden that stimulates the senses
with touchy-feely plants and scented flowers. There are free
open-air barbecue areas near the tower.
www.leipzig-gohlis.de Ⓝ Tram: 3, 7, 12, 16

Waldstrasse Quarter

Slender townhouses with shady inner courtyards cluster in the
streets fanning out from Waldstrasse, the epicentre of Leipzig's
Jugendstil (art nouveau) movement. Once home to the city's
well-to-do fur traders, many of these imposing 19th-century
houses have been restored to their former glory.
www.leipzig-gohlis.de Ⓝ Tram: 4

Zentralstadion Leipzig (Leipzig Central Stadium)

A cool €85 million was spent on creating Leipzig's state-of-
the-art stadium in time for the FIFA World Cup 2006.
The gigantic steel-and-glass structure forms a perfect oval,
accommodating up to 45,000 fans, and boasts the latest
technology. A must for football freaks, the venue also hosts
a wide range of other sporting events and concerts. If you

● *The sumptuous rococo glamour of Gohlis Palace*

want to catch a game here, it's wise to book tickets well in advance, as they are in great demand.

ⓐ Am Sportforum 2–3 ⓣ 0341 234 1100 (ticket hotline)
ⓦ www.sportforum-leipzig.de ⓔ office@arena-leipzig.com
Ⓝ Tram: 3, 4, 7, 13, 15

Zoo

A magnet to families, Leipzig's zoo promotes itself as being eco-friendly but it's got a way to go. The zoo is split into themed lands; while some animals have enough space, others are kept in small enclosures, and the practice of getting elephant Voi Nam to perform soccer tricks is questionable. Young children love the adventure playgrounds and petting area.

ⓐ Pfaffendorfer Strasse 29 ⓣ 0341 593 3500 ⓦ www.zoo-leipzig.de ⓔ office@zoo-leipzig.de ⓛ 09.00–19.00 (summer), 09.00–17.00 (winter); admission charge Ⓝ Tram: 12, 16

CULTURE

Arena

Just a few paces from the stadium, this bright and modern arena reels in the crowds with an eclectic programme. Playing host to major sporting events, concerts, galas and conventions, the venue has space for up to 12,000 people and stages everything from glittering West End musicals and Holiday on Ice spectacles to volleyball and tennis championships.

ⓐ Am Sportforum 2–3 ⓣ 0341 234 1100 (ticket hotline)
ⓦ www.sportforum-leipzig.de ⓔ office@arena-leipzig.com
Ⓝ Tram: 3, 4, 8, 15

Gohliser Schlösschen (Gohlis Palace)

Built for prosperous merchant Caspar Richter in 1756, this sumptuous rococo residence stages cultural events and is a great setting for opera, theatre and classical music. Inside glimpse the Oesersaal's elaborate frescoes and the Steinsaal's vaulted ceilings.

ⓐ Menckestrasse 23 ⓣ 0341 589 690 ⓦ www.gohliser-schloss.de
ⓔ gohliser-schloss@web.de ⓝ Tram: 4, 12

Schiller House

Explore this whitewashed 18th-century farmhouse, where famous poet, philosopher and dramatist Friedrich Schiller lived in 1785, and was inspired to pen '*An die Freude*' (Ode to Joy), and

⬥ *Schiller's 18th-century home*

which houses a small collection of paintings and letters, plus Schiller's silk waistcoat. You can catch an open-air concert here in summer.

🅰 Mencke Strasse 42 🛈 0341 566 2170 🅦 www.leipzig-gohlis.de/schillerhaus 🕑 10.00–18.00 Mon–Sun (summer), 10.00–16.00 Wed–Sun, closed Mon–Tues (winter); admission charge Ⓝ Tram: 4, 12

RETAIL THERAPY

Flakon This tiny shop appeals to foodies, featuring shelves lined with gourmet products from fine wines and liqueurs to raspberry vinegar and courgette chutney. 🅰 Waldstrasse 32 🛈 0160 180 5749 🕑 10.00–19.00 Mon–Fri, 09.00–14.00 Sat, closed Sun Ⓝ Tram: 4

Natur & Fein Organic is the word on shoppers' lips at this health-conscious store, well stocked with eco-friendly cosmetics, Ayurveda products, fresh fruit and vegetables, locally produced wines, crusty bread, honey – and a tempting antipasti selection in case you're planning a picnic in the park.
🅰 Waldstrasse 23 🛈 0341 999 9885 🅦 www.natur-und-fein.de 🕑 10.00–20.00 Mon–Fri, 10.00–16.00 Sat, closed Sun Ⓝ Tram: 4

Ostprodukte A real blast from the past, this cult shop offers a taste of bygone days with a range of East German products, including much-loved tinned brands, toys, postcards and road signs. Look out for the multicoloured Trabi car in front.

ⓐ Waldstrasse 25 ⓦ www.ostprodukte.de
ⓔ info@ostprodukte.de ⓒ 09.00–18.00 Mon–Fri, 09.00–13.00
Sat, closed Sun ⓝ Tram: 4

TAKING A BREAK

Biergarten im Rosental £ ❶ One of the only places you can rest
your feet in Rosental Park, this café is conveniently located next
to the zoo and has a shady beer garden. Prices are reasonable.
ⓐ Pfaffendorfer Strasse 29 ⓣ 0341 583 2503 ⓦ www.zoo-
leipzig.de ⓒ 11.00–19.00 Mon–Sun ⓝ Tram: 12, 16

Café Krüger £ ❷ Open 365 days a year, this cosy café has pretty
much every homemade cake, flan and pastry you could wish for,
from chocolaty Sachertorte to cherry-rich Black Forest gateau.
Forget the diet, it's all far too yummy... ⓐ Delitzscher Strasse 96
ⓣ 0341 911 9145 ⓦ www.café-krueger-leipzig.de ⓒ 07.00–22.00
Mon–Fri, 10.00–22.00 Sat–Sun ⓝ Tram: 14, 16

Mücken Schlösschen £ ❸ A huge leafy beer garden overlooks
the canal at this castle-like building with turrets and towers.
After a long walk in the Rosental, pull up a chair beside the
fountain to drink Bavarian Paulaner beer and snack on white
sausages slathered in mustard. ⓐ Waldstrasse 86 ⓣ 0341 983
2051 ⓦ www.mueckenschloesschen-leipzig.de ⓒ 11.00–19.00
Mon–Sun ⓝ Tram: 4

Sehbrücke Restaurant £ ❹ Join the locals at this friendly
gastro-pub offering value-for-money light meals like chilli con

carne and goulash, washed down with bittersweet Schwarzbier.
ⓐ Wilhelm-Plesse-Strasse 12 **ⓣ** 0341 481 7303 **ⓦ** www.leipzig-gohlis.de/sehbruecke **ⓛ** 17.00–open end Tues–Sat, 10.00–22.00 Sun **ⓝ** Tram: 12

Softeis £ ❺ Hear the ice-cream machines hum at this spotless gelateria, where passionate owner Eugen Hendrich whips up his own soft scoop creations. Try homemade cherry, peach and yoghurt varieties, or relax and watch the world go by from the tiny terrace. **ⓐ** Waldstrasse 38 **ⓛ** 12.00–20.00 Mon–Sun **ⓝ** Tram: 4

Sontag & Dünkel £ ❻ This unassuming little bakery opposite St Michael's Church serves a hearty breakfast for around €3 that includes as much tea or coffee as you can drink. **ⓐ** Nordplatz 7 **ⓣ** 0341 564 7255 **ⓛ** 06.00–18.00 Mon–Fri, 07.00–16.00 Sat, 07.00–12.00 Sun **ⓝ** Tram: 12

AFTER DARK

Restaurants

Frida la Mexicana £ ❼ Fiery Mexican flavours are on the menu at this restaurant, decked out in bright pinks and blues. As the name suggests, the owner has a penchant for Frida Kahlo's work, and larger-than-life portraits of the artist decorate the walls.
ⓐ Waldstrasse 64 **ⓣ** 0341 308 6477 **ⓦ** www.frida-la-mexicana.de **ⓛ** 17.00–01.00 Mon–Sun **ⓝ** Tram: 4

La Locanda £ ❽ Savour well-prepared antipasti, pizza and pasta at this intimate Italian restaurant, affording views to

Friedenskirche church from the attractive terrace.
🅐 Gohliser Strasse 42 🕿 0341 689 4745 🆆 www. la-locanda.com
🅔 info@la-locanda.com 🕒 12.00–14.30, 17.30–23.00 Sun–Fri,
17.30–23.30 Sat 🚋 Tram: 12

Ofenrohr £ ❾ A decent choice for al-fresco dining in summer,
this laid-back place serves wholesome fare like Saxon
Sauerbraten (beef pot roast) with mounds of red cabbage. If
you'd prefer something more international, dishes range from
rabbit to lamb curry. 🅐 Gohliser Strasse 13 🕿 0341 564 9777
🕒 11.30–24.00 Mon–Sun 🚋 Tram: 12

Trattoria No 1 £ ❿ Hundreds of wine bottles line the shelves at
this authentic trattoria, boasting a cavernous cellar. The design
is simple but elegant, and specialities range from seafood
linguine to freshly baked pizza. 🅐 Waldstrasse 64 🕿 0341 211
7098 🕒 11.30–14.30, 18.00–24.00 Mon–Fri, 18.00–24.00 Sat &
Sun 🚋 Tram: 4

Vitha Thai £ ⓫ Wind chimes tinkle as you enter this mirrored
restaurant, decorated with lanterns and tiles. Sample aromatic
Thai, Chinese and Korean dishes, from coconut-rich curries to
steaming plates of noodles with crispy duck. 🅐 Wettiner Strasse
10 🕿 0341 222 9949 🕒 11.30–14.30, 17.30–23.00 Tues–Sun, closed
Mon 🚋 Tram: 4

Gohliser Schlösschen ££ ⓬ Posh with a capital P, this palatial
restaurant is all cream leather, vaulted ceilings and arched
windows. The chef uses seasonal produce to create specialities

like veal carpaccio in tomato vinaigrette and mascarpone figs with rosemary. ⓐ Mencke Strasse 23 ⓣ 0341 561 2992 ⓦ www.restaurant-im-gohliserschloss.de ⓛ 12.00–14.00, 18.00–22.00 Tues–Sun, closed Mon Ⓝ Tram: 4, 12

La Mirabelle ££ ⓭ French cuisine is served with finesse in this art nouveau restaurant. Enjoy mussels in wine or Roquefort gratin on the terrace. ⓐ Gohliser Strasse 11 ⓣ 0341 590 2981 ⓦ http://la-mirabelle.de ⓛ 11.00–15.00, 17.30–24.00 Mon–Fri, 17.30–24.00 Sat–Sun Ⓝ Tram: 12

Bars

Die Gohliserwirtschaft A terrace shaped like a ship complete with decking, fishing nets and lanterns welcomes you to this nautical-themed pub in summer. In winter take a pew at a chunky wood table to drink local brews and eat Leipziger Allerlei stew. ⓐ Gohliser Strasse 20 ⓣ 0341 564 4033 ⓦ www.gohliser.de ⓔ wirtschaft@gohliser.de ⓛ 11.00–01.00 Mon–Sun Ⓝ Tram: 12

Gosenschenke Ohne Bedenken Dating back to 1899, this traditional Gosenschenke inn has won a string of awards as one of Germany's best pubs and beer gardens. Oozing musty charm, the wood-panelled cellar serves a long list of Gose beer varieties and specialities like Gose-Häppchen (pickled camembert and gherkins) and Gosebraten (Gose-marinated beef). ⓐ Mencke Strasse 5 ⓣ 0341 566 2360 ⓦ www.gosenschenke.de ⓔ info@gosenschenke.de ⓛ 17.00–01.00 Mon–Fri, 12.00–01.00 Sat, 12.00–24.00 Sun Ⓝ Tram: 4, 11

Mega Bar Relaxed and unpretentious, this local haunt is a pleasant spot for a quiet beer and snack. The comfortable café-cum-bar doubles as a free WiFi hotspot. ⓐ Gohliser Strasse 19 ⓣ 0341 583 1188 ⓔ info@mega-bar.de ⓛ 09.00–open end ⓝ Tram: 12

⬥ *Go for a Gose at this traditional inn*

THE GOLDEN GOSE

It would be sacrilege to visit Leipzig without trying at least one glass of gold-hued Gose beer at a traditional inn like Ohne Bedenken. This tangy, top-fermented wheat beer takes its name from the Gose stream, which flows through the town of Goslar to the west of Leipzig. For a beer with a twist, order a *Sonnenschirm* (parasol) laced with fruit syrup, a *Frauenfreundlicher* (ladies' friend) with a shot of cherry liqueur, or a *Regenschirm* (umbrella) with a dash of *Kümmel* liqueur.

The city's tipple of choice has an intoxicating history, stretching back 1,000 years to when Emperor Otto III sung the beer's praises. In medieval times it was brewed in Goslar and finally came to Leipzig in 1738, where it became the preferred brew of the *Studiosen* (students), among them Goethe and Schiller. Under Communist rule (1949–90), the beer disappeared from the scene.

With a dedicated passion for Gose, Dr Harmut Hennebach gave the beer a new lease of life when he reopened Ohne Bedenken in 1990. Today, the lightly acidic beer is brewed according to a traditional recipe, with coriander and salt, and sold in long-necked bottles. Leipzig legend still has it that a stroll in the Rosental followed by a Gose beer (or three) is all you need in life to be happy and healthy.

● *Cathedral entrance at Halle bids visitors 'Welcome'*

Halle

Handel, Goethe and Martin Luther all waxed lyrical about Halle, a vibrant university city built high on the riches of its 'white gold' – salt. Climbing medieval castles, cruising the River Saale and chilling on the tower-framed market square, it isn't hard to see why.

GETTING THERE

Located 40 km (25 miles) to the northwest of Leipzig, it's easy to reach Halle by public transport. Frequent Deutsche Bahn train connections link the two cities, just half an hour's journey apart. If you're driving, take the A14 motorway.

● *Cruising the River Saale*

SIGHTS & ATTRACTIONS

Alter Markt
Hemmed in by half-timbered and Renaissance houses, this square was once home to Halle's wealthy salt merchants. In the centre is the Eselbrunnen (Donkey Fountain).
ⓐ Alter Markt ⓝ Tram: 2, 5

Boating the River Saale
Hire a canoe or rowing boat to explore the River Saale, or board a 20-km (12^1/$_2$-mile) tour to Wettin. If you're lucky, you'll spot a swamp beaver.
ⓐ Riveufer 10 ⓣ 0151 1720 9964 ⓦ www.bootsverleih-wiederhold.de ⓛ 10.00–19.00 Mon–Sun (Apr–Oct) ⓝ Tram: 7, 8

Botanischer Garten (Botanical Gardens)
The 300-year-old botanical gardens nurture 12,000 species.
ⓐ Am Kirchtor 3 ⓣ 0345 552 6271 ⓦ www2.biologie.uni-halle.de ⓛ 14.00–18.00 Mon–Fri, closed Sat & Sun (Apr–Oct); admission charge ⓝ Tram: 7

Burg Giebichenstein (Giebichenstein Castle)
Clinging to rocks above the River Saale, this 10th-century fortress is all silvery turrets and thick curtain walls. Roam the foundations and vaults at the open-air museum. The surrounding parkland affords fine river views.
ⓐ Seebener Strasse 1 ⓣ 0345 523 3857 ⓛ 09.00–18.00 Tues–Fri, 09.00–18.30 Sat & Sun, closed Mon (Apr–Oct); admission charge ⓝ Tram: 7.

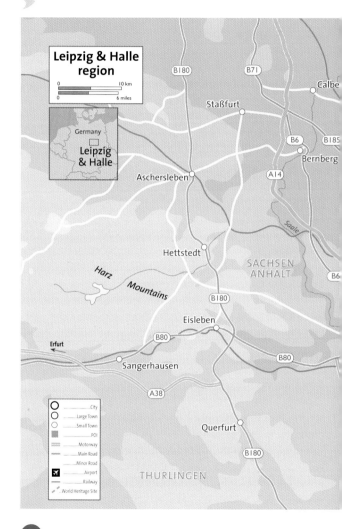

Leipzig & Halle region

0 — 10 km
0 — 6 miles

Germany

Leipzig & Halle

B180

B71

Calbe

Staßfurt

B6

B185

Bernberg

A14

Aschersleben

Saale

Hettstedt

SACHSEN ANHALT

B6

Harz Mountains

B180

Eisleben

Erfurt

B80

B80

Sangerhausen

A38

○ City
○ Large Town
○ Small Town
■ POI
Motorway
Main Road
Minor Road
✈ Airport
Railway
World Heritage Site

Querfurt

B180

THÜRINGEN

Dom (Cathedral)

Originally part of a Dominican monastery, Halle's early Gothic cathedral impresses with its baroque art and Peter Schro sculptures. ⓐ Dom Platz Ⓝ Tram: 2, 9, 10

Franckesche Stiftung (Francke Foundations)

One of Germany's key cultural landmarks, this vast 17th-century orphanage comprises 25 institutions including a museum, library and music school. A must-see is the Cabinet of Curiosities, sheltering everything from fine art to whale bones.
ⓐ Franckeplatz 1 ⓣ 0345 2127 450 Ⓦ www.francke-halle.de
Ⓛ 10.00–17.00 Tues–Sun, closed Mon; admission charge
Ⓝ Tram: 2, 5, 9

Marktkirche (Market Church)

Peer up at the four towers crowning this late Gothic church, where Martin Luther the Reformer once preached – his death mask is located in the sacristy. Step inside to admire Renaissance art and the organ on which Handel played his first notes.
ⓐ An der Marienkirche 2 ⓣ 0345 517 0894
Ⓦ www.marktkirche-halle.de Ⓝ Tram: 2, 5, 9

Marktplatz (Market Square)

All streets lead to Halle's huge market square. Glimpse the five towers dominating the skyline, the bronze Handel monument and the Marktschlösschen's blushing bricks and gables.
ⓐ Marktplatz Ⓝ Tram: 2, 5, 9

CULTURE

Beatles Museum

A shrine to the singing Liverpudlians, this museum is crammed with Beatles memorabilia.

ⓐ Alter Markt 12 ☏ 0345 290 3900 ⓦ www.beatlesmuseum.net
🕓 10.00–20.00 Wed–Sun, closed Mon & Tues; admission charge
Ⓝ Tram: 2, 5

Händel-Haus (Handel House)

See where master composer George Frideric Handel was born. The collection of 700 instruments includes a Flemish harpsichord and 17th-century lute, while manuscripts, paintings and artefacts offer an insight into Handel's life.

ⓐ Grosse Nikolaistrasse 5 ☏ 0345 5009 0411
ⓦ www.haendelhaus.de 🕓 09.30–17.30 Mon–Sun Ⓝ Tram: 2, 5

Kulturinsel (Culture Island)

The eclectic programme at Halle's cultural enclave moves from cutting-edge plays to dancing marionettes.

ⓐ Grosse Ulrichstrasse 50–51 ☏ 0345 205 00
ⓦ www.kulturinsel-halle.de Ⓝ Tram: 2, 7

Landesmuseum für Vorgeschischte (National Museum for Prehistory)

This fascinating museum houses 10 million artefacts from dinosaur bones to a primitive man's fossilised remains. The Bronze Age Nebra Sky Disc is the world's oldest chart of the heavens.

Richard-Wagner-Strasse 9 ● 0345 524 730
www.landesmuseum-fuer-vorgeschichte-halle.de
09.00–19.30 Tues, 09.00–17.00 Wed–Fri, 10.00–18.00 Sat &
Sun, closed Mon; admission charge ● Tram: 7

● Handel's birthplace is now a fascinating museum

Opernhaus Halle (Opera House)

Halle's neoclassical opera house stages opera, operetta, ballet, musicals and cabaret.

🅐 Universitätsring 24 🅣 0345 511 00 🅦 www.opernhaus-halle.de 🕒 10.00–20.00 Mon–Sat, closed Sun (ticket office) 🅝 Tram: 1, 2, 5, 7, 9

Stiftung Moritzburg (Moritzburg Art Gallery)

Sitting on 500 years of history, this red-turreted castle showcases 19th- and 20th-century artworks. Keep an eye open for Expressionist works by Otto Mueller and Edvard Munch.

🅐 Friedemann-Bach-Platz 5 🅣 0345 212 590 🅦 www.moritzburg.sachsen-anhalt.de 🕒 11.00–20.30 Tues, 10.00–18.00 Wed–Sun, closed Mon; admission charge 🅝 Tram: 1, 2, 5, 7, 9

Technisches Halloren- und Salinemuseum (Technical Saltworks Museum)

Housed in a beautiful half-timbered building, this former Prussian saltworks traces Halle's history, with demonstrations and displays of original costumes and equipment.

🅐 Mansfelder Strasse 52 🅣 0345 209 3230 🕒 10.00–17.00 Tues–Sun, closed Mon; admission charge 🅝 Tram: 4, 9

TAKING A BREAK

Bücher-Café La Lit £ Warm terracotta tones and squishy sofas give this café on the market square a relaxed feel.

🅐 Marktplatz 3 🅣 0345 293 7202 🕒 09.30–20.00 Mon–Fri, 09.30–18.00 Sat, closed Sun 🅝 Tram 2, 5

Café Schade £ Baked according to a centuries-old family recipe, the cakes at this 400-year-old patisserie near the river make mouths water and waistlines expand.  Seebener Strasse 20  0345 523 1551  09.00–18.00 Mon–Sun  Tram 8, 12

Eiscafe Florenz £ Floor-to-ceiling glass lets light flood into this Italian café, a nice spot to refuel.  Leipziger Chaussee 147  0345 688 8902  09.00–20.00 Mon–Sat, 14.00–18.00 Sun  Bus: 43

Il Rospo £ Chocoholics indulge their cravings at this tiny café which prides itself on using organic, seasonal ingredients.  Burgstrasse 4  0345 682 4464  08.00–18.00 Mon–Fri, 10.00–18.00 Sat & Sun  Tram: 7

Krug zum Grünen Kranze £ This riverside café has entrancing views of Giebichenstein Castle.  Talstrasse 37  0345 299 8899  www.krugzumgruenenkranze.de  Tram: 7

AFTER DARK

Restaurants
Matador £ This authentic Argentinian restaurant serves prime Black Angus beef. Try the South American speciality, *matambre* (beef strips, corn and pumpkin).  Geiststrasse 32  0345 678 4443  www.steakhaus-matador.de  17.00–23.00 Mon–Fri, 11.30–14.30, 17.00–24.00 Sat, 11.30–22.00 Sun  Tram 3, 7, 8, 10

Mönchshof £ Beamed ceilings and murals set the scene in this Hallemarkt restaurant. The terrace has views of the Göbel-

Brunnen fountain. Talamtstrasse 6 0345 202 1726 www.moenchshof-halle.de Tram: 2, 5, 9

Palaiss £ Whether you fancy a spicy stir-fry, sausage salad or seafood paella, this beautiful red-brick restaurant with riverside terrace comes up with the goods. Ankerstrasse 3c 0345 977 2651 www.palaiss.de 18.00–open end Mon–Sat, from 10.00 Sun Tram: 2, 9

Sushi am Opernhaus £ The décor is minimalistic, the ingredients fresh and the clientele laid-back in this Japanese restaurant. August-Bebel-Strasse 3–5 0345 681 6627 www.sushifreunde.de 11.30–14.00, 18.00–22.00 Mon–Fri, 18.00–23.00 Sat, 18.00–22.00 Sun Tram: 2

Zum Ritter £ Go back to medieval times at this castle-like restaurant, where you can grill skewered kebabs over hot lava stones and drink steins of beer as folk music plays. Sternstrasse 7 0345 294 3027 11.00–open end Mon–Sun Tram: 2, 5

Zur Schnitzelwirtin £ Sunny yellow walls and 70 different kinds of *Schnitzel* make this a top choice for carnivores with big appetites. Grosse Märkerstrasse 18 0345 202 9938 www.schnitzelwirtin.de 11.00–23.00 Mon–Sat, 11.00–15.00 Sun Tram: 2, 5

Bars & clubs
Enchilada Halle's party people head here for jumbo margarita cocktails, tequila shots and Mexican beer. Happy hour is from

18.00 to 21.00.  Universitätsring 6  0345 686 7755  www.enchilada.de  halle@enchilada.de  Tram: 7

Mo's Daniels Trendies sink into the chocolate-brown leather sofas at this sleek café-cum-bar serving late-night snacks.  Bernburgerstrasse 1  0345 686 9800  www.mosdaniels.de  Tram: 8

Turm Set in Moritzburg's stone ramparts, this club hosts some of Halle's hottest parties and stages events from rock concerts to dance productions. Sit in the torch-lit beer garden in summer.  Friedemann-Bach-Platz 5  0345 202 3737  www.turm-net.de  Tram: 7

Zanzibar This popular haunt's alcoholic smoothies – Mocha Orange and French Connection, for instance – take some beating.  Universitätsring 6a  0345 686 7420  www.zanzi-bar.de  11.00–open end Mon–Fri, 16.00–open end Sat & Sun  Tram: 7

ACCOMMODATION

Jugendherberge Halle £ Near the Opera House, this central youth hostel offers the cheapest digs in town. Located in a pretty villa, dorms are spacious and clean.  August-Bebel-Strasse 48a  0345 202 4716  www.jugendherberge.de  jh-halle@djh-sachsen-anhalt.de  Tram: 2, 5

City-Hotel am Wasserturm ££ The modern, light-flooded rooms at this peaceful hotel are a good base for exploring the banks of the River Salle by bike or on foot. @ Lessingstrasse 8 @ 0345 298 20 @ www.cityhotel-halle.de @ Tram 12

Dormotel Halle ££ Near the main station, this hotel offers contemporary rooms. Enjoy breakfast in the frescoed dining room or on the terrace. @ Delitzscher Strasse 17 @ 0345 57 120 @ www.dormotel-halle.de @ info@dormotel-halle.de @ Tram: 7, 9

Galerie Hotel Esprit ££ Expect a warm welcome and personalised service at this arty hotel. The 19th-century terracotta-coloured house doubles as a gallery, staging regular exhibitions. @ Torstrasse 7 @ 0345 212 200 @ www.esprit-hotel.de @ info@esprit-hotel.de @ Bus: 27

Hotel Am Ratshof ££ This whitewashed townhouse near the market square features a 15th-century vaulted cellar and leafy beer garden. Spacious rooms have comfy beds and a hearty breakfast is included in the price. @ Rathausstrasse 14 @ 0345 202 5632 @ www.hotel-am-ratshof.de @ info@hotel-am-ratshof.de @ Tram 1, 2

CHARMING CHIMES

If you don't see it, you'll hear it! Soaring 84 m (275 ft) above the market square, the Roter Turm (Red Tower) houses the world's biggest carillon. The 246 spikes punctuating the spire are said to ward off evil spirits. Built in 1506, this freestanding bell and clock tower's glockenspiel comprises 76 bells. Get there on the hour to hear them chime.

Dessau-Wörlitz Gartenreich

In this UNESCO World Heritage Site, you can be spotting beavers by the lake one minute and sipping B52s in a trendy bar the next. Welcome to a wilderness with an urban edge.

GETTING THERE

The speedy A14 and A9 motorways link Leipzig to the Dessau-Wörlitz Gartenreich, a 50-minute drive away. There are good and frequent Deutsche Bahn train connections to Dessau.
If you're travelling to Wörlitz, take bus number 333 from Dessau's bus station.

SIGHTS & ATTRACTIONS

Bauhaus Dessau

An awesome block of concrete, glass and steel designed by Bauhaus director Walter Gropius, this is a prime example of the kind of creations that emanated from the German art school in the 1920s. Each space is designed differently, so allow time to take in the whole building.
🚊 Gropiusallee 38 📞 0340 650 8251 🌐 www.bauhaus-dessau.de
✉ besuch@bauhaus-dessau.de 🕐 10.00–18.00 Mon–Sun; admission charge 🚍 Bus: 10, 11

Fürst Franz Path

Hire your own set of wheels from Dessau's main station to pedal this 60-km (37$^1/_2$-mile) trail slicing through the

Gartenreich. Flitting from one palace and garden to the next, pause to explore Grosskühnau and Georgium.

ⓐ Mobilitätszentrale, Dessau ⓣ 0340 213 366 ⓛ 09.00–17.00 Mon–Fri, 09.00–14.00 Sat, closed Sun

Gotisches Haus

With its turrets, towers and peaches-and-cream interior, this neo-Gothic mansion is the architectural equivalent of a wedding cake. Watch the light hit the Rittersaal's magnificent stained-glass windows or come in the evening to see them illuminated.

ⓐ Wörlitz ⓛ 10.00–18.00 Tues–Sun, closed Mon (May–Sept), 10.00–18.00 Sat & Sun (Apr & Oct); admission charge

ⓝ Bus: 333

Grosskühnau

Retreat to this English-inspired landscape garden and reed-fringed nature reserve, hugging the banks of Lake Kühnau. Picnic beside gentle slopes of vines and catch a glimpse of Giacobo Pozzi's Italian-designed Vineyard House – a snippet of Tuscany in Saxony-Anhalt!

ⓐ Schloss Grosskühnau, Dessau ⓣ 0340 646 150

ⓦ www.gartenreich.com ⓝ Bus: 10, 11

Lake Wörlitz

Swap Venice for Wörlitz's shimmering lake and canals aboard a brightly painted gondola. The 45-minute tour takes in highlights such as the Gotisches Haus.

ⓐ Schloss Wörlitz ⓣ 0349 052 0216 ⓛ 10.00–18.00 (May–Sept), 11.00–16.00 (Oct–Apr) ⓝ Bus: 333

Luisium

Surrounded by open countryside, Luisium Palace fuses Classical and neo-Gothic elements. Take a peek at the banqueting hall's murals, then relax in the flower-strewn gardens.

ⓐ Schloss Luisium, Dessau ⓘ 0340 218 3711
ⓦ www.gartenreich.com ⓛ 10.00–18.00 Tues–Sun, closed Mon (summer), 10.00–17.00 Tues–Sun, closed Mon (winter); admission charge ⓝ Bus: 13

Meisterhäuser (Master's Houses)

These cube-shaped houses are where Bauhaus masters like Walter Gropius, Oskar Schlemmer, Wassily Kandinsky and Paul Klee once lived and worked. A highlight is the colourful Kandinsky/Klee House, where the walls are painted 170 different shades.

ⓐ Ebertallee, Dessau ⓘ 0340 661 0934
ⓦ www.meisterhaeuser.de ⓛ 10.00–18.00 Tues–Sun, closed Mon (Feb–Oct), 10.00–17.00 Tues–Sun, closed Mon (Nov–Jan); admission charge ⓝ Bus: 10, 11

Middle Elbe Biosphere Reserve

This expansive floodplain forest beckons nature lovers. Hiking or biking, you'll pass half-moon lakes, woodlands and meadows. But the big draw is the endangered beaver. The beaver enclosure observation deck is the best place to spot them. The Auenhaus information centre provides more details.

ⓐ Auenhaus, Dessau ⓘ 0349 044 0610
ⓦ www.biosphaerenreservatmittlereelbe.de
ⓔ bioresme-info@t-online.de ⓛ 10.00–17.00 Mon–Fri,

11.00–17.00 Sat & Sun (May–Oct), 10.00–16.00 Mon–Fri, 13.00–16.00 Sat & Sun (Nov–Apr)

Oranienbaum

Sniff out fragrant citrus trees in Europe's longest orangery. A highlight is the Chinese garden with its octagonal pagoda and stone bridges. The baroque palace shelters Dutch treasures from tapestries to blue-and-white ceramics.

ⓐ Oranienbaum ⓣ 0349 042 0259 ⓦ www.oranienbaum.de
ⓒ 10.00–18.00 Tues–Sun, closed Mon (Feb–Oct), 10.00–17.00 Tues–Sun, closed Mon (Nov–Jan); admission charge ⓥ Bus: 331, 333

◭ Take to the water at Lake Wörlitz

Schloss Mosigkau (Mosigkau Palace)

Princess Anna Wilhelmine of Anhalt-Dessau poured pots of her daddy's money into building this sublime rococo palace, adorned with Rubens paintings and baroque furniture, and complete with a mind-boggling maze.

🅐 Knobelsdorffallee 3, Dessau 🅒 0340 52 1139
🅦 www.gartenreich.com 🅛 10.00–18.00 Tues–Sun, closed Mon (summer), 10.00–17.00 Tues–Sun, closed Mon (winter); admission charge 🅝 Tram: 3, Bus: 16

🔺 Rococo rapture at Schloss Mosigkau

Schloss Wörlitz (Wörlitz Palace)

This grand 18th-century palace was the summer residence of Prince Leopold III. His royal jewels include Rubens originals and English ceramics. The palace overlooks the mirror-like Lake Wörlitz.

ⓐ Wörlitz ⓣ 0349 052 0302 ⓦ www.gartenreich.com
ⓛ 10.00–17.00 Tues–Sun, closed Mon (summer), 10.00–17.00 Tues–Sun, closed Mon (winter); admission charge ⓝ Bus: 333

Tierpark Dessau

Come eye-to-eye with brown bears and alpacas at Dessau's zoo, set in leafy grounds near the station.

ⓐ Querallee 8, Dessau ⓣ 0340 614 426 ⓦ www.tierpark. dessau.de ⓔ info@tierpark.dessau.de ⓛ 09.00–18.00 (summer), 09.00–dusk (winter); admission charge ⓝ Train: main station

CULTURE

Anhalt Theatre

Dessau's columned theatre stages philharmonic orchestra performances, opera, operettas, musicals, plays, ballet and puppet theatre for younger audiences.

ⓐ Friedensplatz 1a, Dessau ⓣ 0340 25 110
ⓦ www.anhaltisches-theater.de ⓝ Tram: 1, 3

Georgium (Anhalt Art Gallery)

A stroll through these sculpture-dotted landscape gardens on the River Elbe's banks leads to the Anhalt Art Gallery, housed in Georgium Palace. The picture gallery's 2000-strong collection includes masterpieces by Dutch and Flemish Masters.

ⓐ Puschkinallee 100, Dessau ⓣ 0340 6612 6000
ⓦ www.georgium.de ⓔ info@georgium.de ⓛ 10.00–17.00
Tues–Sun, closed Mon; admission charge ⓥ Bus: 10, 11

RETAIL THERAPY

Galerie Bauart Take home your own bit of Bauhaus from
Dessau's interior design gallery: there are some nifty design
knick-knacks that won't break the bank. ⓐ Gropiusallee 81,
Dessau ⓣ 0340 661 0246 ⓦ www.galerie-bauart.de ⓛ 12.00–
18.00 Fri, Sat & Sun ⓝ Bus: 10, 11

Hofladen An obligatory picnic stop, this shop is crammed with
locally sourced organic produce like freshly pressed apple juice,

⬤ *The royal palace of Wörlitz*

mustards, honey, sausages and creamy goat's cheese.
ⓐ Pötnitz 6, Dessau-Mildensee ❶ 0340 21 940
ⓦ www.mildenseer-hofladen.de ❷ 09.00–18.00 Tues–Fri,
09.00–12.00 Sat, closed Sun

TAKING A BREAK

Gaswirtschaft im Küchengebäude £ Right next to Wörlitz Palace,
munch on spit-roasted wild boar by an open fire or sip beer on
the cobbled terrace. ⓐ Am Wörlitzer Schloss ❶ 0349 052 2338
ⓦ www.bruhnke-woerlitz.de ❷ 11.00–18.00 Mon–Tues, 11.00–
21.30 Wed, Thur & Sun, 11.00–22.30 Fri & Sat ⓝ Bus: 333

Klub im Bauhaus £ Take a bite out of Bauhaus at this shrine to
1920s design. Nibble pastries with an espresso on white plastic
stools or enjoy tapas with a nice glass of red on the terrace.
ⓐ Gropiusallee 38, Dessau ❶ 0340 650 8444 ⓦ www.
klubimbauhaus.de ❷ 09.00–24.00 Mon–Sun ⓝ Bus: 10, 11

Moni's Café £ Sticky pastries and delicious handmade cakes
forbid you to count calories at this snug café. ⓐ Neue Reihe 179,
Wörlitz ❶ 0349 052 0124 ❷ 10.00–17.00 Mon–Sat, 14.00–17.00
Sun ⓝ Bus: 333

AFTER DARK

Restaurants
Brauhaus zum Alten Dessauer £ The menu is meaty at this
wood-beamed brewery and beer garden. Feast on roast pork

knuckles with a glass of amber-hued Alter Dessauer beer.
 Lange Gasse 16, Dessau 0340 220 5909 www.alter-dessauer.de 11.00–24.00 Mon–Sun Tram: 1, 2

Kartofflekäfer £ From fiery Hungarian potato soup to Peruvian potato stew, this place gives culinary credit to the humble potato. Neue Reihe 149, Wörlitz 0349 052 0509 www.kartoffelkaefer-woerlitz.de 11.00–23.00 Mon–Sun Bus: 333

Kornhaus Restaurant £ Soak up River Elbe views through the glass windows of this sphere-shaped Bauhaus restaurant, where a granary once stood. Kornhausstrasse 146, Dessau 0340 640 4141 www.kornhaus.de info@kornhaus.de 11.00–23.00 Mon–Sun Bus: 10, 11

Tokyo Haus ££ Sushi fans tuck into well-prepared fish and vegetarian specialities at this contemporary Japanese restaurant. Elisabethstrasse 41, Dessau 0340 661 5918 www.tokyo-haus.de 11.30–14.30, 17.00–23.00 Tues–Fri, 12.00–23.00 Sat & Sun Tram: 1, 3

Bars & clubs
Chaplins A head-spinning cocktail list, mellow grooves and cheap prices tempt at this New York-style bar.
 Wolfgangstrasse 14, Dessau 0340 220 0444 www.starsdiner.de 18.00–02.00 Mon–Sun Tram: 3

Cup & Cino Serving Dessau's frothiest cappuccino and freshest salads, this Italian-style café transforms into a funky bar by night, where DJs spin lounge music. ⓐ Zerbster-Strasse 30, Dessau ⓣ 0340 250 8869 ⓦ www.cupcino.com ⓛ 09.00–01.00 Mon–Sat, 10.00–01.00 Sun ⓝ Tram: 1, 2

Kiez Café Drawing a young crowd, this chilled café stages plenty of events. Happy hour is from 20.00 to 22.00. ⓐ Bertolt-Brecht-Strasse 29, Dessau ⓣ 0340 212 032 ⓛ 20.00–01.00 Mon–Sun ⓝ Tram: 1

Projekt 1 Come here to relax with cocktails on the black-and-cream leather benches. ⓐ Zerbster-Strasse 2, Dessau ⓣ 0340 230 1230 ⓛ 18.00–01.00 Mon–Sun ⓝ Tram: 1

ACCOMMODATION

Adria £ A sound choice for water babies and the budget conscious, this lakeside campsite has spacious, shady pitches right beside Lake Mildensee. There's an onsite bistro, barbecue area, laundry and playground. ⓐ Dessau-Mildensee ⓣ 0340 230 4810 ⓝ Bus: Strandbad Adria

Heuhotel £ For back-to-nature fun, head for Wörlitz's hay hotel. This wood-beamed barn is full to the brim with lovely soft hay, where you'll sleep sweetly and very cheaply. You can rent a sleeping bag for a couple of euros. ⓐ Neue Reihe 149, Wörlitz ⓣ 0349 052 0509 ⓦ www.kartoffelkaefer-woerlitz.de ⓔ woerlitz6@aol.com ⓝ Bus: 333

Jugendherberge Dessau £ Directly on the Elbe cycling trail, this Dessau youth hostel is surrounded by trees. The excellent

facilities include a terrace, table tennis, basketball and bike hire.
ⓐ Waldkaterweg 11, Dessau ⓣ 0340 619 452 ⓦ www.
jugendherberge.de ⓔ jh-dessau@djh-sachsen-anhalt.de ⓝ Bus: 11

Zum Hauenden Schwein ££ Recently renovated from top to
bottom, this hotel has bags of character. The rooms evoke a
country cottage with floral prints and squishy beds.
ⓐ Erdmannsdorffstrasse 69, Wörlitz ⓣ 0349 053 0190
ⓦ www.pension-zum-hauenden-schwein.de ⓝ Bus: 333

> ### CALLING CULTURE VULTURES …
> The best way to discover compact Dessau is to walk the
> Culture Trail, taking in Dessau's key sights such as the
> Bauhaus, Anhalt Theatre, Georgium Palace and the neo-
> Renaissance town hall. The bronze signs on the pavement
> will help you find your way. The tourist office provides
> free maps. ⓐ Zerbster Strasse 2c ⓣ 0340 204 1442
> ⓦ www.dessau.de

▶ *The Leipzig tourist information centre*

Directory

GETTING THERE

By air

A number of airlines operate a frequent, direct service between Leipzig-Halle Airport and 60 European destinations including London, Paris and Vienna. A 20-minute journey from the centre of Leipzig, the modern airport offers a full range of services.

Air Berlin  www.air-berlin.com
Germanwings www13.germanwings.com
Ryanair www.ryanair.com

Many people are aware that air travel emits CO_2, which contributes to climate change. You may be interested in the possibility of lessening the environmental impact of your flight through the charity Climate Care, which offsets your CO_2 by funding environmental projects around the world. Visit www.climatecare.org

By car

Germany's roads are well maintained, although the lack of a speed limit on motorways means it can get a bit fast and furious at times. Driving is on the right. If possible, it's wise to avoid morning and evening rush hours (07.30–09.00 and 16.00–18.00).

By rail

Leipzig's gleaming main station has excellent connections on high-speed ICE trains to major German cities including Berlin,

Frankfurt, Munich and Hamburg. Deutsche Bahn provides information on routes and timetables.

Deutsche Bahn Ⓦ www.bahn.de

By bus

National Express and Eurolines operate a Europe-wide service and pull into Leipzig's main bus station in front of the main station.

National Express Ⓦ www.nationalexpress.com

Eurolines Ⓦ www.eurolines.com

ENTRY FORMALITIES

Documentation

EU, Australian, Canadian, New Zealand and United States citizens must have a valid passport to enter Germany, but do not require a visa for stays of less than 90 days. If you are arriving from another country, you may need a visa and should contact your consulate or embassy before departure. The German Embassy provides more information on entry requirements at Ⓦ www.auswaertiges-amt.de

Customs

It is free to import goods worth up to €175 from a non-EU country, but you should check restrictions on the imports of tobacco, perfume and alcohol. Further information is available from the German customs website Ⓦ www.zoll.de

MONEY

The national currency is the euro (€), broken down into 100 cents. Coins are in denominations of 1, 2, 5, 10, 20 and 50 cents, and of

1 and 2 euro. There are banknotes of 5, 10, 20, 50, 100, 200 and 500 euro.

There are plenty of ATMs in central Leipzig where you can withdraw cash with a credit or EC card 24 hours a day. Banks are normally open 09.00–18.00 from Monday to Thursday and 09.30–16.00 on Friday. Main branches like Deutsche Bank on Augustsplatz do not close for lunch.

You'll find bureaux de change in banks, airports and the main station. Banks usually offer the best currency exchange rates. Most bureaux de change, travel agencies and hotels accept euro traveller's cheques for cashing.

Around 60 per cent of Leipzig's shops, restaurants, bars and hotels accept major credit cards, so it's worth checking before you pay. It's wise to carry a small amount of cash just in case.

HEALTH, SAFETY & CRIME

Leipzig is a safe city to visit and there are no particular health risks. No immunisations or health certificates are required and the tap water is safe to drink.

Medical care is of a high standard in Germany. Pharmacies (*Apotheken*) can treat minor ailments and usually open 09.00–18.00 Monday to Friday and 09.00–12.00 Saturday. Your hotel should be able to arrange for you to see an English-speaking doctor, if necessary.

EU citizens are entitled to free or reduced-cost emergency health care in Germany with a valid European Health Insurance Card (EHIC), which entitles you to state medical treatment but does not cover repatriation or long-term illness. There is a charge for routine medical care. All travellers should invest in a good health insurance policy before visiting.

The crime rate in Leipzig is low. While they are in a minority, members of the extreme right (neo-fascists) have been associated with violent outbursts towards those they consider 'foreign', so it's wise to keep your wits about you. If you are the victim of a crime, you should inform the police by calling 110 (see *Emergencies*).

OPENING HOURS
Shops
Most shops open 09.00–20.00 Mon–Fri and 09.00–16.00 Sat. Some open on Sundays in the tourist areas. Major shopping malls like the Hauptbahnhof stay open daily until 22.00.

Banks
Banks generally open 09.00–18.00 Mon–Thur and 09.30–16.00 Fri. All close at weekends, but many have 24-hour ATMs.

TOILETS
Leipzig has a number of clean public toilets in the centre. Most are accessible for travellers with disabilities and offer baby-changing facilities. You'll need €0.50 to unlock the door at the city's 24-hour automatic toilets. If you need to freshen up on arrival, the shower at the main station costs around €7. Most restaurants, bars and large stores have facilities for customers.

CHILDREN
There is plenty to keep tots and teens on their toes in Leipzig, from free play in the huge parks and gardens to boating

Plagwitz's canals and riding horses through the Auenwald forest. In the summer, take your kids to Lake Cospuden or Lake Kulkwitz to splash in clear waters, let off steam on the beach or go to the zoo. A 50 per cent reduction is usually offered for children, and kids are welcome in most restaurants and cafés. Drugstores in the city centre like DM and Müller stock everything from nappies to organic baby food. Most stores and public toilets have clean baby-changing facilities.

The LVB group ticket for up to five people offers great value for money on Leipzig's public transport network. Kids aged 6 to 13 years travelling alone get special discounts. www.lvb.de

Fischer-Art's bright murals enliven the city

Child-friendly attractions include:

Belantis

Just south of Leipzig, kids love the rides, roller coasters and giant pirate ship at this theme park. Family tickets are available.

ⓐ Zur Weissen Mark 1 ⓦ www.belantis.de

ⓔ willkommen@ belantis.de 🕓 10.00–18.00 Mon–Sun (Apr–Oct); admission charge 🚋 Tram: 3

Euro Eddy's Family Fun Centre

This huge indoor adventure playground keeps boredom at bay with its slides, ball pits, bumper cars and climbing walls.

ⓐ Kastanienweg 1 🕿 0341 940 6244 ⓦ www.euroeddy-leipzig.de

ⓔ info@euroeddy-leipzig.de 🕓 14.00–20.00 Mon–Fri, 10.00–20.00 Sat & Sun; admission charge 🚌 Bus: 129

COMMUNICATIONS
Phones

Leipzig's modern public telephone boxes are glass with a grey and pink strip. Only a handful of these accept coins (minimum charge of €0.20), so you'll need to purchase a prepaid phone card from a newsagent, post office, station or T-Punkt store. These are available in denominations of €5, €10 and €20. Alternatively, many of the city's internet cafés double up as call centres and offer good deals on international calls.

To call Leipzig, dial 0049 for Germany, then 341 for Leipzig followed by the four- to seven-digit number. To call out of Germany, simply dial 00 followed by the country code and the local number. For example, for Britain this is 0044.

National Directory Enquiries ☎ 11833, or 11837 for an English-speaking service
International Directory Enquiries ☎ 11834

Post

Stamps are sold in post offices and some newsagents. It costs €0.70 to send a standard letter or postcard to Europe, and by airmail to North America, Australia, South Africa and New Zealand it is €1.70. In addition to normal postal services, most post offices stock a good range of stationery, have ATMs and occasionally a bureau de change. The main post office in the city centre is on Augustusplatz. ⓦ www.deutschepost.de

Internet

Internet cafés have sprouted up all over the centre recently. Expect to pay between €1.50 and €3 for an hour online. Some cafés and bars with AOL terminals offer free, limited access for customers, including 100 Wasser and Barfusz on Barfussgässchen, and Bar Central on Nikolaistrasse. Other popular centres are:

Click Planet ⓐ Lauchstädter Strasse 20 ☎ 01805 445 745 235 ⓦ www.clickplanet.de ⏱ 10.00–20.00 Mon–Fri, 09.00–14.00 Sat
Intertelcafé ⓐ Brühl 64 ☎ 0341 462 5879 ⓦ www.intertelcafe.de ⏱ 10.00–22.00 Mon–Sun
Le Bit ⓐ Rosa-Luxemburg-Strasse 32 ☎ 0163 2982 092 ⓦ www.le-bit.de ⏱ 09.00–03.00 Mon–Fri, 10.00–03.00 Sat & Sun
Trixom ⓐ Härtelstrasse 21 ☎ 0341 33 98 661 ⓦ www.trixom.de ⏱ 09.00–03.00 Mon–Fri 10.00–03.00 Sat & Sun

WiFi hotspots

Wireless internet access (WiFi) has become widespread in Leipzig, with a fair share of cafés, restaurants and bars offering it on their menu – sometimes free for customers. Try:

Albert's Restaurant, Café & Bar ⓐ Markt 9
Bagel Brothers ⓐ Nikolaistrasse 42
Buddha Art Gallery ⓐ Neumarkt 9-19
CAM Café am Markt Bar ⓐ Katharinenstrasse 2
Leipzig-Halle Airport ⓐ Terminalring 11
Leipzig Hauptbahnhof ⓐ Willy-Brandt-Platz 5

ELECTRICITY

The electricity system in Germany is very reliable. It is 230 volts, 50 Hertz (round, two-pin plugs). Visitors from the UK and US will need adaptors.

TRAVELLERS WITH DISABILITIES

Leipzig caters to travellers with special needs. Most of the city's key attractions are wheelchair-friendly, featuring ramps, accessible toilets and low-level lift buttons. Among the best are the Old Town Hall, the Grassi Museum Complex, the Fine Arts Museum, Leipzig Museum, the Monument to the Battle of the Nations and Botanical Gardens. Many offer concessions (*Ermässigung*) for visitors with disabilities.

Good restaurant choices for travellers with disabilities include the Bachstüb'l, Auerbachs Keller, Bayerischer Bahnhof and the beer garden at Ohne Bedenken.

Wheelchair-accessible toilets are located in Clara-Zetkin-Park, Augustusplatz, Karl-Liebknecht-Strasse and Goethestrasse.

Germany: NATKO (National Tourism Coordination Agency for All People e. V.) ☎ 0211 33 68 001 ⓦ www.natko.de ⓔ info@natko.de

United Kingdom and Ireland: British Council of Disabled People (BCDP) ☎ 01332 295551 ⓦ www.bcodp.org.uk

USA and Canada: Society for Accessible Travel & Hospitality (SATH) ☎ 212 447 7284 ⓦ www.sath.org
Access-Able ⓦ www.access-able.com

Australia and New Zealand:
Accessibility ⓦ www.accessibility.com.au
Disabled Persons Assembly @ 04 801 9100 ⓦ www.dpa.org.nz

TOURIST INFORMATION
Dessau Tourist Information
Book accommodation, tickets and guided city tours at Dessau's tourist office. @ Zerbster Strasse 2c ☎ 0340 204 1442
ⓦ www..dessau.de ⓔ touristinfo@dessau.de ⏰ 09.00–18.00 Mon–Fri, 09.00–13.00 Sat (summer), 09.00–17.00 Mon–Fri, 10.00–13.00 Sat (winter)

German National Tourist Office
Well-designed, this site is a mine of information. Brochures can be ordered online. ⓦ www.germany-tourist.de

Halle Stadmarketing
Browse leaflets, pick up maps and book accommodation at Halle's helpful little visitor centre. @ Leipziger Strasse 105/106

ⓣ 0345 122 9984 ⓦ www.stadtmarketing-halle.de
ⓔ touristinfo@stadtmarketing-halle.de ⓛ 09.00–19.00
Mon–Fri, 10.00–16.00 Sat, 10.00–14.00 Sun

Leipzig Erleben

This visitor centre offers insightful themed tours of Leipzig and the surrounding area. ⓐ Richard-Wagner-Strasse 1 ⓣ 0341 7104 230 ⓦ www.leipzig-erleben.com ⓔ info@leipzig-erleben.com ⓛ 10.00–18.00 Mon–Fri, 09.00–16.00 Sat, 10.00–14.00 Sun

Leipzig Tourist Service e.V.

Leipzig's friendly and helpful tourist office provides information, maps, timetables, souvenirs and an accommodation and ticket booking service. ⓐ Richard-Wagner-Strasse 1 ⓣ 0341 7104 265 ⓦ www.leipzig.de ⓔ Info@LTS-Leipzig.de ⓛ 10.00–18.00 Mon–Fri, 09.00–16.00 Sat & Sun

Saale Tourist

This tourist office provides information on the Saale region, from art and culture to events and accommmodation. ⓐ Alter Markt 2, Halle ⓣ 0345 470 1480 ⓦ www.saale-tourist.de ⓔ info@saale-tourist.de ⓛ 09.00–19.00 Mon–Fri, 10.00–16.00 Sat, 10.00–14.00 Sun

Visit Saxony

This comprehensive site gives an overview of Saxony and you can order brochures online. ⓣ 0351 491 700 ⓦ www.saxonytourism.com ⓔ info@sachsen-tour.de

Emergencies

The following are national free emergency numbers:

Police ℹ 110
Fire & ambulance ℹ 112
Breakdown (ADAC) ℹ 0180 222 2222

When you dial the European emergency number 112, ask for the service you require and give details of where you are, what the emergency is and the number of the phone you are using. The operator will connect you to the service you need.

POLICE

Each of Germany's 16 states has its own police force (*Landespolizei*). The Federal Government police force is called the (*Bundespolizei*); it patrols at airports, train stations and country borders. Police officers in Germany wear green uniforms, although this is gradually being phased out in favour of blue uniforms like most other EU police forces.

MEDICAL

It is strongly recommended to have a valid health insurance policy before travelling to Germany. EU citizens are entitled to free or reduced-cost emergency health care with a European Health Insurance Card (EHIC). Pharmacies (*Apotheken*) are usually open 09.00–18.00 Monday to Friday and 09.00–12.00 Saturday. In case of accident or illness call ℹ 112

CONSULATES & COUNCILS

UK British Council ⓐ Beethovenstrasse 15 ☏ 0341 339 8968
ⓦ www.britishcouncil.de

USA American Consulate General ⓐ Wilhelm-Seyfferth-Strasse 4
15 ☏ 0341 213 8425 ⓦ www.usembassy.de
ⓔ amcongenirc@pd.state.gov

EMBASSIES

UK ⓐ Wilhelmstrasse 70–71, Berlin ☏ 030 204570
ⓦ www.britischebotschaft.de ⏰ 09.00–17.30 Mon–Fri
USA ⓐ Clayallee 170, Berlin ☏ 030 2385 174
ⓦ http://berlin.usembassy.gov ⏰ 08.30–12.00 Mon–Fri
Australia ⓐ Wallstrasse 76–79, Berlin ☏ 030 700 129 129
ⓦ www.australian-embassy.de ⏰ 09.00–11.00 Mon, Wed & Fri
Canada ⓐ Leipziger Platz 17, Berlin ☏ 030 20312 0
ⓦ www.canada.de ⏰ 08.00–12.30, 13.30–17.00 Mon–Fri
Republic of Ireland ⓐ Friedrichstrasse 200, Berlin ☏ 030 2385 174
ⓦ www.botschaft-irland.de ⏰ 09.30–12.30, 14.30–16.45 Mon–Fri
South Africa ⓐ Tiergartenstrasse 18, Berlin ☏ 030 220720
ⓦ www.suedafrika.org

EMERGENCY PHRASES

Help! Hilfe! *Heelfe!*   **Fire!** Feuer! *Foyer!*   **Stop!** Halt! *Halt!*

Call an ambulance/a doctor/the police/the fire service!
Rufen Sie bitte einen Krankenwagen/einen Arzt/die Polizei/
die Feuerwehr!
*Roofen zee bitter inen krankenvaagen/inen artst/dee
politsye/dee foyervair!*

INDEX